WITHDRAWN

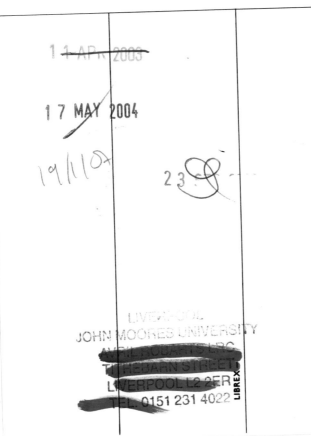

Oxford University Press, Great Clarendon Street, Oxford OX2 6DP
Oxford   New York
Athens Auckland Bangkok Bombay Calcutta Cape Town
Dar es Salaam Delhi Florence Hong Kong Istanbul Karachi
Kuala Lumpur Madras Madrid Melbourne Mexico City
Nairobi Paris Singapore Taipei Tokyo Toronto
and associated companies in
Berlin Ibadan

Oxford is a trade mark of Oxford University Press

Published in the United States
by Oxford University Press Inc., New York

First published June 2002 by **Oxford University Press** for
The International Institute for Strategic Studies
Arundel House, 13–15 Arundel Street, Temple Place, London WC2R 3DX
www.iiss.org

Director John Chipman
Editor Mats R. Berdal
Copy Editor Anne-Lucie Norton

British Library Cataloguing in Publication Data
Data available

Library of Congress Cataloguing in Publication Data

ISBN 0-19-851674-6
ISSN 0567-932x

Contents

Glossary

ACP	Africa Caribbean Pacific (countries)
ANC	African National Congress
ASEAN	Association of Southeast Asian Nations
ASSIST	Assistance to Support Stability in Service Training
CALDH	Centre for Legal Action on Human Rights
CIVPOL	United Nations Civilian Police
CPP	Cambodian People's Party
DAC	Development Assistance Committee (of the OECD)
DDA	Department of Disarmament Affairs (of the UN)
DFID	Department for International Development (of the UK)
DPA	Dayton Peace Agreement
EU	European Union
FALINTIL	the armed forces for the liberation of East Timor
FCO	Foreign and Commonwealth Office
GTZ	Deutsche Gesellschaft für Technische Zusammenarbeit
ICITAP	International Criminal Investigative Training Assistance Programme
IMF	International Monetary Fund
MoD	Ministry of Defence (UK)
NATO	North Atlantic Treaty Organisation
NGO	non-governmental organisation
NOA	National Orientation Agency (of Nigeria)
OECD	Organisation for Economic Cooperation and Development

OHR	Office of the High Representative (of the United Nations)
ONUMOZ	United Nations Operation in Mozambique
ONUSAL	United Nations Observer Mission in El Salvador
OSCE	Organisation for Security and Cooperation in Europe
RJB	(Resor javne bezbednosti) Public Security Department of the Serbian Ministry for the Interior
SDA	The Party for Democratic Action (of Bosnia and Herzegovina)
SEECAP	Southeast Europe Common Assessment Paper on Regional Security Challenges and Opportunities
SFOR	Stabilisation Force in Bosnia and Herzegovina
SSR	Security Sector Reform
TNI	Indonesia's armed forces
UNDP	United Nations Development Programme
UNMIK	United Nations Interim Administrative Mission in Kosovo
UNTAC	United Nations Transitional Authority in Cambodia
UNTAES	United Nations Transitional Authority in Eastern Slavonia
USAID	United States Agency for International Development
WOLA	Washington Office on Latin America

Introduction

Over the past ten years, the frequent collapse of formally agreed peace accords, the failure to set countries emerging from conflict on a path of sustainable development, and the rise in the number of so-called 'failed states', have all focused attention on the role of the security sector as an obstacle, but also a potential and indeed inescapable partner, in efforts to establish lasting peace in countries and regions ravaged by protracted armed conflict. The security sector of a state may be defined broadly as encompassing those elements that have been granted a legitimate and exclusive role in the exercise of coercive power in society to deal with external and internal threats to the security of the state and its citizens. As such, security sector reform (SSR) encompasses all those organisations that have the authority to use, or order the use of force, or the threat of force, as well as those civil structures that are responsible for their management. The organisations concerned include: military and paramilitary forces; intelligence services; police forces, both national and local, together with border guards and customs services; judicial and penal systems; and the civil authorities mandated to control and oversee these agencies.[1] It is the growing recognition of the importance of this sector for the effective transition from war to peace that explains the current interest in SSR, especially among Western donor countries. This paper examines the background to the debate, as well as the policy implications for donors and institutions raised by the challenge of reform.

Why has there been such an interest in the SSR agenda since the mid-1990s, and why have external actors taken the approach they have? The short answer to the first part of the question is that for international and Western institutions the security sectors of states emerging from conflict or undergoing other forms of rapid change are increasingly hard to avoid. International protectorates such as Kosovo and East Timor, peace agreements negotiated with a high level of external involvement such as those in Cambodia, El Salvador, Bosnia or Palestine, the aid–trade relationship that Western states have with much of Africa and the Pacific, the expansion of European regional organisations, and the reassessment of security relationships after the Cold War, have all brought external actors face to face with the consequences of factionalised, wrong-sized, dictatorial, non-professional security sectors. As for the character of external involvement, this can be understood as deriving from dissatisfaction with the lack of progress of previous development agendas on the part of Western donors, and the changing expectations by which contemporary involvement with security by these donors is characterised. Expectations now include a sustainable peace, conflict prevention and increased regional and international cooperation. The holistic viewing of the security sector that the SSR agenda promises, encompassing as it does both structural and normative elements, is the way to fulfil these expectations, its proponents argue.

The SSR agenda is therefore a simultaneously compelling and challenging enterprise. This is reflected in both its popularity and track record to date. SSR is a much-used phrase. From international institutions such as the UN or World Bank to individual government ministries, such as those of the UK, USA and Germany, or regional groupings such as the EU or NATO, everyone is interested in, or at least promoting, SSR. The confidence with which the objectives of the SSR agenda are proclaimed contrasts however with the rather limited nature of reform successes so far. Attempts to operationalise reform have often been plagued by political unrest and uncertainty in the states in question, institutional reluctance to change within pre-existing security forces, corruption and economic scandals, lack of societal ownership of reform, and damaging inconsistencies on the part of external reformers. In other words, actual engagement in reform has so far fallen far short of the expectations that the SSR agenda promotes.

The SSR agenda itself is characterised by numerous conceptual shortfalls. While there is consensus among policy-makers that the biggest challenge to the consolidation of peace and development involves a consideration of the broader set of issues raised in the SSR agenda, and general agreement about the technical demands that the agenda raises, there remain serious conceptual gaps when it comes to considering how to operationalise these demands. Sustained critical thinking about how best to engage in reform contexts is lacking. For example, while it is fashionable to think about SSR 'from below', privileging local ownership and the role of civil society, little has been said or done about what this means practically. Just what are the implications of local ownership for external engagement? How can reform partnerships best be established and sustained? How can existing political structures be used to encourage more inclusive security arrangements? What are the opportunities and limitations of external assistance in influencing the relationship between the state and civil society? Is political change a prerequisite for effective external involvement in reform? Or, put another way, if there is no apparent self-help available is there anything that reformers can or should do? What can reformers achieve by imposing reform? Moreover, insofar as the SSR agenda appears to presume a state capable of effective policy, does this mean that a functioning state is necessary for sustainable reform? Is it possible to prioritise aspects of the SSR agenda at the expense of others or is sequencing of reform not always an option?

Given the complexities raised by these questions, there is an understandable desire on the part of donors to manage risk – primarily to themselves – and to control the environment within which they are operating. There is a tendency to narrow operational terrain to protect donors' interests, to portray reform goals as tangible in order to gain donor support, and to make them fail-safe by setting boundaries that can be moved, thus jeopardising the holistic argument upon which the SSR agenda itself is based. It is worth remembering that there have in fact been many arguments for implementing and attempts to implement comprehensive approaches in the quest for sustainable peace in the past. Democratisation, good governance, peace building, reconstruction and nation building are some of the more notable efforts, mostly associated with the work of multilateral bodies such as the UN, the IMF and the World Bank. How, then, does SSR relate to these approaches? Even if SSR can be integrated with these broader strategies, can it overcome the political problems – both those that external actors bring with them and those of the reform contexts themselves – that previous approaches (less explicitly focused on the security sector) could not?

The argument in this paper is not that SSR, as it has been developed and practiced, is inevitably bound to fail but that it does remain an underdeveloped concept. While the SSR agenda is more than just an exercise in re-labelling, it is still characterised by a collection of undifferentiated and often ill-defined strategies. While there is much discussion about capabilities for reform and its technical requirements, there has been insufficient analysis of how to mobilise such resources. In short, while the objectives of SSR and its general motivations may be laudable, there exists a critical policy vacuum when it comes to engaging effectively with the key issues raised by these objectives and the reform agenda as a whole.

This paper seeks to address this core SSR problem by asking three central questions:

- How have external approaches to SSR evolved and what do they entail technically?
- What specific problems does the SSR agenda face operationally?
- What concrete policy recommendations for engagement can be drawn from reform experiences to date?

The first chapter explores the origins and objectives of the SSR agenda. It examines its core assumptions, the theoretical and international contexts within which these can be understood, and general trends in the SSR debate to date. A survey of these SSR discussions reveals that although it is possible to draw up a list of the technical dimensions that comprise the SSR agenda – politically, institutionally economically, socially, and operationally – debate about actually putting these demands into practice is under developed. Both international actors and Western donors alike draw up a list of similar institutions and groups that may need to be reformed and agree that such reform should follow certain principles, but there has been little critical debate about how best to engage in reform and address the specific challenges that may exist in reform contexts. As Chalmers points out, the difficulties of the SSR agenda lie not so much in the identification of the problem, 'but in the nature of the proposed solution'.[2] These difficulties are most keenly felt during attempts to operationalise SSR, and form the core discussion of Chapter 2.

The contexts in which reform is attempted cover a vast array of security situations. These range from states undergoing transitions from authoritarian rule, such as Nigeria, Indonesia, Russia and Ghana, to states consolidating their independence, often following some form of authoritarian rule, such as Croatia, Slovenia, Ukraine and Georgia, to post-settlement territories such as Northern Ireland, Bosnia, Kosovo, Sierra Leone and Mozambique. Newly established states or states in the process of emerging, such as Palestine and East Timor are included.[3] Despite important differences in the historical and political backgrounds of these examples, Chapter 2 identifies a number of key themes present in the security sectors of all cases that pose both crucial questions and dilemmas when it comes to effecting reform. These structural and behavioural problems are considered in relation to the different dimensions that comprise the SSR agenda.

Despite the operational difficulties external assistance in SSR has encountered to date, it is possible to identify areas and means for implementing specific, concrete reforms that fit in with the overall holistic ethos that the SSR agenda promotes. The final chapter sets these forth in terms of three stages of policy recommendations. First, the pre-implementation stage focuses on policy planning. Second, the implementation stage focuses upon the points of entry for external actors in reform contexts and the ways in which local ownership of the reform process can be achieved. Third, the consolidation stage is concerned with sustaining and building on reform efforts, and verifying reform progress.

Chapter 1

The Security Sector Reform Agenda

The SSR agenda is rooted in the search for solutions to the challenges faced by multilateral and bilateral donors concerned with development and peace consolidation in the aftermath of the Cold War. A survey of these actors' responses to such challenges illustrates both the vital need to find a way to address and reframe security in the immediate post Cold War era, and also how in the attempts to do so some of the key questions that affect external assistance in security reform have been neglected or overlooked.

This chapter explores the origins and objectives of the SSR agenda. It gives a brief survey of the debates and discussions that led to the birth of the concept. These fall into three main categories, each grouped around a particular set of actors and concerns: the UN and its role in peace agreements and international administrations; the EU, NATO and the eastward enlargement of the European security community; and the extensive involvement of development agencies in shaping policy within developing countries. Despite the differences between these three groups of actors, the solutions that they propose and the ways in which they view the development–security relationship, their approaches are remarkably convergent. This is reflected in the birth of the SSR agenda in the first place and the ability to draw out its main requirements. However, as the final part of this chapter illustrates, while it is relatively easy to draw up such a check-list for the SSR agenda, it is much more difficult to see how that summary can be implemented. This problem is the result of a policy vacuum in the SSR debate to date.

Traditional Security Sector Involvement

External interest in the security sectors of other states has a long history. Colonisation by European states necessitated involvement with the security arrangements of other regions, even if there were not always security forces *per se*. In addition, US involvement in the security concerns of Latin America and the Caribbean dates back to the beginning of the twentieth century and aimed to provide greater security to its own borders. During the Cold War, military assistance was a significant instrument of US and Soviet foreign policy, involving *inter alia*, the supply of military equipment and training to governments and opposition movements that were seen to be serving their broader geopolitical interests.

Partly as a consequence of the large number of military coups in Latin America, Africa and Asia in the 1960s and concern that the resources consumed by the military could be better employed for other purposes, development actors also became involved in security assistance operations. With the decolonisation process underway, it was sometimes hoped that the military might play a role in uniting people and building modern nations. However, these arguments further legitimised the ongoing extensive military assistance programmes. For example, the support provided to third world countries by the USSR was founded almost entirely on arms exports and training for the armed forces or underground movements. In the United States, France and the UK, where military assistance was sometimes declared as development cooperation, it at times dwarfed actual development cooperation. The focus remained fixed upon military training and the supply of weapons, rather than structural reform.

By the late 1960s, development involvement with both the armed forces and police assistance dwindled. The positive image of the military as state modernisers changed when the predicted rapid development failed to occur. Not until the final stages of the Cold War, with the second wave of democratisation in the 1980s, did development thinking actively return to the security debate. This time, through the emergence of concepts such as professionalisation and good governance, conflict prevention and peace building, and support for demobilisation and post-conflict reconstruction, concern was focused on how to bring the armed forces under civilian control. It was the experience gained in implementing these initiatives, accompanied by dramatic indigenous changes in the security arrangements of developing country states, which represented the immediate precursors to the SSR agenda of the mid-1990s.

The end of the Cold War brought with it a significant reorienting of the security priorities of Western states. A different, but not necessarily novel, group of problems took centre stage. These ranged from civil conflicts, religious and ethnic extremism, and mass population displacements, to all-encompassing concerns, such as economic inequality and environmental degradation. At the same time, a number of largely indigenous security sector changes spanning every continent, were already underway. The fall of military regimes in Latin America meant that military institutions were brought under the control of national executives and legislatures. These transitions were also accompanied by the growing prominence of issues of public order in the wake of rising crime rates in that region. Foreign interventions in Haiti and Panama removed old militaries from power, necessitating the emergency restructuring of new internal security forces. In El Salvador a negotiated end to the civil war produced a government commitment to police reform, backed by international verification and assistance.[1]

In South Africa the question of civilian governance became an issue of hot debate following the 1994 election of President Nelson Mandela. The restructuring of South Africa's armed forces was accompanied by a recognition that changes in the security sector more generally were a major priority for the new multiracial government. The main features of the emerging policy framework included the reallocation of resources from defence towards citizen security and development objectives. The interim constitution paid careful attention to issues of democratic control of the security forces, as well as their roles and functions.[2] Meanwhile, the collapse of the Soviet Union necessitated attempts to reshape the security institutions of numerous Central and Eastern European states. In South-east Asia, the 1997 financial crisis (combined with the political crisis in Indonesia) had important effects on the security sectors of the region. Procurement funds were reduced, forcing both a re-evaluation of defence modernisation plans and a reduction of the military's role in decision-making.[3]

Post-Cold War Security Involvement: Donor Responses

The impact of these dramatic transitions, and the instability with which some were accompanied, combined with a re-evaluation of what was possible and useful in the changing political climate, produced a different way of viewing and dealing with security. Western donors and international institutions were first to voice the articulation of this changing view. International interventions that directly engaged with the security sectors of states recovering from, or involved in, civil wars, became more numerous, costly and open-ended affairs. International military forces sought to achieve sustainable peace, ethnic reconciliation and future conflict prevention, with a greater emphasis upon developmental rather than strategic goals. The way in which the words 'security' and 'sector' were given meaning changed markedly towards a more holistic interpretation, encompassing both civilian and military aspects and, most crucially, questions of how the security sector was governed. The security challenges they faced and the approaches used in dealing with these challenges are discussed below.

The United Nations: Peace Agreements and International Administrations

In the first half of the 1990s regional peace initiatives and global disarmament led to a number of peace accords which stipulated procedures for the controlled reduction of troops and the economic reintegration of former combatants. Special programmes for the demobilisation and reintegration of combatants were widely recognised as a key factor in peace building. These initiatives often developed around UN peacekeeping operations and post-war reconstruction programmes whose aim was the implementation of a comprehensive peace settlement that would address all the elements necessary to achieve sustainable peace based upon sound development principles.

For example, the Paris Agreements signed in late October 1991 mandated the UN Transitional Authority in Cambodia (UN-TAC) to 'exercise power in political, military, economic and other functional domains', ranging from 'the organizing and conducting of elections to coordinating the repatriation of Cambodian refugees; from disarming and demobilizing military forces of warring parties to guaranteeing the Cambodian people's human rights; from coordinating a major program of economic and financial support for rehabilitation and reconstruction to stopping outside military assistance and verifying the total withdrawal of foreign forces.' Such unprecedented authority for a UN peacekeeping force was heralded as a 'systematic effort at nation-building.' Not only did such a mandate illustrate a shift towards a development focus, but it also brought the issue of development back into the wider security debate. Other important operational experiences included the UN Transitional Administration in Eastern Slavonia (UNTAES) and the UN Operation in Mozambique (ONUMOZ). While the latter was not mandated to assume direct control of certain aspects of the civil administration, as was the case in Cambodia, it was responsible for supervising the overall implementation of a comprehensive peace settlement, including the disarmament, demobilisation and reintegration of ex-combatants into civil society.

Demobilisation efforts undertaken by UN Missions were accompanied by calls for more holistic thinking as it was realised that there was no necessary correlation between reductions in force levels and military budgets and the success of economic development of a country. While such reductions were accompanied by a redirection of resources towards development goals and an increase in political stability on some occasions (South Africa, Zimbabwe and Namibia during the post-election period), there were also cases where ill-considered security sector restructuring programmes contributed to an increase in political instability and worsened civil–military relations, such as in Eritrea, the Central African Republic, the former Zaire and Sierra Leone. Coinciding with the greater attention being given to the security-development relationship, in 1992 the UN Civilian Policing Department was established with a specific mandate to assist in the reform of police forces in countries in transition from war to peace.

Over time, the UN Development Programme (UNDP) began to emphasise the inherent relationship between development and justice.[4] In 1994 UNDP introduced the notion of 'human security' to describe this shift in programme concerns. Reflecting upon the fact that failure to ensure accountability of security forces resulted in renewed abuses in some post-war settings such as Rwanda, Somalia and Haiti, the office set up projects in its missions in Africa and Latin America designed to create politically acceptable distributions of power by addressing countries' legal frameworks and political and military boundaries. UNDP also became a major player in reintegration programmes in Central America, Cambodia, Burundi, Tajikistan, and Angola. In Guatemala the office focused on accelerating and strengthening the placement of the civilian police force and promoting pilot projects for the creation of 'judicial centers,' one-stop shops where citizens can find the police, the local judge and magistrates and legal assistance. UNDP and the UN's department of Disarmament Affairs (DDA) began to cooperate closely in West Africa and elsewhere in the provision of operational support for efforts leading to the control and collection of small arms.

UN Missions which visited Mali and its neighbouring countries in 1994 and 1995 recommended reforming the police, national guard, *gendarmerie* and customs authority with international assistance in order then to be able to put a stop to the transfer of small arms. This approach was labelled 'security first' as it integrated security problems into development as part of a strategy for sustainable development. The importance of this refocusing of UN operations was heralded in UN reports at the time. For example, according to the Supplement to An Agenda for Peace (1995): 'Demilitarization, the control of small arms, institutional reform, improved police and judicial systems, the monitoring of human rights, electoral reform and social and economic development can be as valuable in preventing conflict as in healing the wounds after conflict has occurred.'[5] The Agenda for Development (1995) linked the establishment of a just and democratic society even more closely to careful attention to the security sector. In 1998 the Secretary-General's report on the causes of conflict and the promotion of durable peace and sustainable development in Africa reaffirmed the importance of the security-development relationship, stating: 'The prevention of conflict begins and ends with the promotion of human security and human development ...'[6] The parallels in thinking with regional institutions at the time are striking.

Changing Regional Relationships: The Enlargement of Europe

European regional institutions emerged as key actors in the reconceptualisation of the security–development relationship, partly as a consequence of their involvement in peace processes, but also as a direct result of the changing regional relationships affecting their own security concerns. For example, with the end of the Cold War, the role of the European Community (as it was known until 1993) changed radically. Many European states emerging from communism looked to the Community for assistance and eventual membership, and an opportunity arose to develop a true European Union (as it was known from 1993). Closer cooperation between the EU and NATO also called for a stable Euro-Atlantic security environment: 'an integrated and democratic Europe without dividing lines.'

Discussions about the enlargement of the EU and NATO were key factors in raising the profile of SSR. The reform of candidate members' security sectors was a condition of eventual membership. EU enlargement not only offered the prospect of European integration, but also demanded that candidate countries of Central and Eastern Europe 'progressively integrate the European model into their own structures' (as the Commission puts it). For example, the 'Working Table on Security Issues' was set up within the EU's Stability Pact for South Eastern Europe (under the auspices of the OSCE) to initiate programmes which would help contribute to the integration of the countries of the region into European and Euro-Atlantic structures. The table deals with issues such as border security, the problem of trafficking in small arms and the reform of the security forces. More specifically, the last category includes reintegration and retraining programmes, destruction of weapons, civilian control of the military forces, review of defence doctrines, transparency in military budgeting and right-sizing of military forces and expenditure, and demining and disaster preparedness and prevention.

The debate on SSR has been further promoted through the emphasis placed by NATO on the fact that membership and cooperation is 'based on shared values'. Candidate countries are required to deal with 'specific challenges in the security field'. These include: illegal armed groups; terrorism; the provision of full accountability of the armed forces to civil society; proliferation and the illegal transfer of weapons. In addition to the reform of the armed forces, the reform of the entire spectrum of security agencies is set forth, including the police, internal troops, border security units and internal security services. Human and civil rights, and the nurturing of civil society are to be promoted and realised through 'democratic governance'. New roles for national armed forces are also described, requiring 'a deep transformation of their structures and doctrines'. The armed forces of countries aspiring to join NATO 'must be able to deal effectively with the full range of missions including collective defence and peace support operations.'[7]

The dividends of such integration are significant. The incentive provided by the prospect of membership of NATO and the EU is seen by these institutions as a key factor in promoting peace, security and stability in the region. More specific issues that could be addressed include: international crime, ethnic conflicts, terrorism, and humanitarian and environmental problems. Potentially, it is hoped that conflict prevention and regional crisis management could be undertaken more effectively. The Southeast Europe Common Assessment Paper on Regional Security Challenges and Opportunities (SEECAP) launched in May 2001, is the first comprehensive common document on perceptions and priorities to 'build a secure, stable and indivisible Euro-Atlantic area'. The SEECAP is intended not only to enhance political openness, but also to promote increased cooperation in defence, security reform, economic and democratic development and environmental protection.[8] NATO has since made repeated calls for security to be conceived in an even broader fashion, including 'conflict prevention and management through targeted actions', and also 'conflict prevention [as] an integral part of Alliance members' external policies, both individually and collectively'. Further, 'security policy must tie together into a coherent whole aimed at conflict prevention, conflict management – whether the latter is carried out through military or non-military means – and post-conflict reconstruction strategies'.[9]

Development Aid and Trade

Emerging in the 1950s and lasting until the 1980s, the post-Second World War development paradigms – reconstruction in the 1950s, development planning in the 1960s, meeting basic human needs in the 1970s, and finally, structural adjustment in the 1980s – were mainly concerned with reducing poverty in the South through the promotion of economic growth based on investment and the application of science and technology. The implicit assumption was that economic development automatically enhanced peace and stability. However, experience demonstrated that this was not necessarily the case: economic development was no guarantee of peace and security. Indeed, without security, the conditions rarely existed for development to take place. Fostering socio-economic development, moreover, meant fostering change, change that could lead to social and political tensions.

Gradually, it became common international ground that development assistance should be deployed with due regard to the existing socio-political frameworks and that it should be deployed in a way that did not intensify tensions in the society. This is generally referred to as the 'do-no-harm' approach. However, apart from the brief sojourn during the 1960s with the military and police, development and security remained separate spheres in donor activities. In the 1990s, these spheres met once again as it was argued that development assistance also had an important and direct contribution to make to conflict prevention and peace consolidation, potentially strengthening peace and stability. Discussion focused on how development assistance could address basic needs in a more targeted and consistent way than in the past. Spurred on by the conspicuous failure of aid in parts of Africa and Latin America, the end of the Cold War represented a pivotal point for the reshaping of the development–security relationship.

The World Bank

Since the early 1990s, the World Bank has been involved in debates on security policy through its analyses on the appropriateness of military expenditure. In 1993 the Bank undertook a pilot study on demobilisation and has since continued its involvement with demobilisation and reintegration programmes. The Post-Conflict Unit was established in 1997, the same year that the Bank's annual report promoted the concept of 'citizen security'. Two years later the Vice-President of the World Bank, Ian Johnson, wrote: 'Just as AIDS, the environment and corruption have become development issues, so human security issues should take a more central place on the development agenda.'[10] The World Bank was quick to back such arguments up with statistics, pointing out that the majority of countries in arrears to the Bank are countries in conflict, that one in five persons are living in a country in conflict, and that 19 of the 20 poorest nations are either actively engaged in civil war or have recently emerged from active hostilities.[11] The Comprehensive Development Framework is designed to take 'a holistic approach to development, highlighting the interdependence of all elements of development – social, structural, human, governance, environmental, economic and financial.'

In particular, the spectrum of activities included in the Bank's legal and judicial reform programmes has expanded considerably since the mid-1990s. Initially its activities aimed to develop legal environments that would encourage local and foreign private investment. When legislation alone failed to produce results, attention turned to the building up of legal infrastructure. Examples of such projects are to be found in Guatemala, Zambia, Cambodia, Armenia, the West Bank and Gaza, Kazakhstan, Peru, Georgia, and Russia. Key elements include: promoting judicial independence through improved appointment, financing and disciplinary procedures; modernising judicial administration; training judges and court personnel; strengthening good governance (including fighting corruption); building capacity in public agencies, supporting bar associations and legal education; and supporting civil society organisations. According to the Bank, 'A well functioning legal and judicial system is critical both as an end in itself as well as a means to facilitate and leverage the achievement of other development objectives ... Poverty cannot be fought and gains cannot be sustained without effective and equitable legal systems.'[12]

The European Union

The EU and its member states provide approximately half of all public aid to developing countries and Europe is their main trading partner in many cases. Ever since the 1960s, the EU has established and built up an increasing series of political and trade relations as well as cooperation agreements with Latin America. In recent years, development assistance has come to be seen as a key instrument in the EU's efforts to address the root causes of conflict. For example, development assistance is directed to projects to improve public security, to build up civil police forces, and to encourage respect for human rights and fight the accumulation and proliferation of small arms.

This new approach, which emphasises the targeted contribution of development assistance to peace building, was also the basis of the negotiations of the Partnership Agreement signed with the Africa Caribbean Pacific (ACP) countries in Cotonou on 23 June 2000. This agreement defines the aid, trade and development relationship between the EU and 77 ACP countries, focusing much more on the political dimension of development than in the past. Respect for human rights, democracy and the rule of law, together with good governance (as a fundamental element), lie at the core of this political dialogue. A new and privileged role is given to civil society and NGOs. The Cotonou Agreement makes explicit the link between development issues and conflict prevention, management and resolution. More specifically, Article 11 of the Agreement sets out a new legal framework and a mandate for the Commission and the Member States to tackle the challenges emanating from crisis-affected countries. It reflects the increasing relevance of the conflict issue to Europe, the proliferation of conflicts in Africa, and the intensification of international debates on the use of development instruments for peace building and conflict prevention.

Conflict prevention – through the promotion of human rights, democracy, the rule of law and good governance – has become an explicit objective of the new European Commission

Development Policy, which focuses on poverty reduction and requires that development assistance should be targeted to address the root causes of violent conflict. The Common Foreign and Security Policy declaration, reached on 11 April 2001, also represents the culmination of a series of discussions about the development–security relationship. In its Annex the Commission pledges to play an increasingly active role in the security sector area. This will take the form of activities aiming at improving police services, promoting conversion, disarmament and non-proliferation and supporting human rights training for the whole security sector.

The Organisation for Economic Cooperation and Development (OECD)

The evolution of security and development thinking has perhaps been most clearly perceptible in the work of the Development Assistance Committee (DAC) of the OECD. The discussion in DAC has broadened in scope from demobilisation and reintegration projects, to landmine clearance, to capacity building of security and justice systems. The DAC became concerned with excessive military expenditure and civil–military relations in aid recipient countries in the early 1990s and produced guidelines for good practice in 1993. In 1997 it established a Task Force on Conflict, Peace and Development and the same year produced a report, 'Military Expenditures in Developing Countries: Security and Development'. The 1997 OECD/DAC 'Guidelines on Conflict, Peace and Development on the Threshold of the 21st Century' stated that: 'Work in war-torn or conflict prone countries must be seen as an integral part of the cooperation challenge … excessive military expenditures and responses to complex emergencies have come to represent a major claim on development cooperation budgets. More basically, helping to strengthen the capacity of a society to manage conflict without violence must be seen as a foundation for sustainable development.' The publication of these guidelines signalled a sea change in the thinking of donors with respect to conflict prevention. Central to the DAC rationale was the need to explore how development cooperation could 'contribute proactively to conflict prevention and post conflict rehabilitation and reconstruction.'

Development Ministries: United States Agency for International Development and Department for International Development

Until after the Cold War development ministries avoided involvement in security sector issues, while security assistance from foreign and defence ministries focused on traditional train-and-equip strategies. Since the early 1990s, concern over the allocation of resources to the security sector and various bilateral ventures in 'peace consolidation' has given national donors an important role in supporting a more holistic development of security sector programs. Foremost among those to develop work in the security sector have been the United States Agency for International Development (USAID) and the UK's Department for International Development (DFID).

USAID's early history of involvement in security reforms was reawakened in the early 1990s by the momentous political transitions occurring in much of the world. From the mid-1990s, the Agency issued numerous reports and launched programs supporting the reform of the police, the military and the judicial sector simultaneously, with the objective of 'creating the underpinnings for strong socio-economic development'. In a report dated April 1997, USAID states: 'Civil–military relations must be linked to security and to democratization ... Security in this context implies dual roles for the military – internal (for public safety) and external (for national defence).'[13] According to USAID in 1998, 'The new security agenda of the post-Cold War period requires a review of civil–military relations that goes beyond the traditional notion of subordination of the armed forces to elected civilian leaders ... There is an urgent need to bring civil–military relations into the development dialogue.'[14]

USAID is quite explicit about the relationship between aid and economic interests. For example, strengthening democracy and open markets in Georgia is described as serving long-term US regional, economic and humanitarian interests. As the western portal to the Great Silk Road and the newest conduit of Caspian oil to world markets, Georgia has become a strategic gateway of energy and trade routes linking east and west. USAID's strategy for Georgia aims to integrate institutional and policy reform at the national level with local and grass-roots capacity building: bolstering civil society, developing democratic local governance, promoting the rule of law and fighting corruption, and undertaking reintegration programmes.

The UK government has also progressively increased its support for security sector reforms since the end of the Cold War. In particular, the administration of Prime Minister Tony Blair has significantly reinforced the trend of linking development to security since assuming office in May 1997, taking the view that poverty eradication cannot succeed without SSR. It has renamed and refocused the military assistance programme – now known as ASSIST, (Assistance to Support Stability In Service Training) – and has created a Defence Diplomacy Mission for the MOD which includes training and education 'to help develop the skills and structures needed by modern, democratically accountable forces'. The government has taken part in increasing numbers of disarmament, demobilization and reintegration programmes. Police assistance has also been undergoing a reorientation since the early 1990s when it was moved from the Foreign and Commonwealth Office (FCO) to the Overseas Development Administration. UK police assistance is increasingly concentrating on strengthening the management capacity of police forces to implement change.[15]

However, it was DFID that made the most explicit and direct connection between development, security and conflict. According to DFID, 'There are two reasons above all why we should embrace the objectives of international development. First, because it is right to do so … . Second, because we have a common interest in doing so … helping strengthen the capacity of a society to manage conflict without violence must be seen as a foundation for sustainable development.' Not only did poverty and underdevelopment come to be associated with conflict, but conflict itself, through the destruction of development assets and social capital, was regarded as complicating poverty and deepening underdevelopment.[16] On 9 March 1999, Secretary of State for International Development, Clare Short, announced a new policy linking poverty and the security sector in a speech at the Centre for Defence Studies, King's College London: 'Security Sector Reform and the Elimination of Poverty'.

The Birth of a Concept

It was out of the discussions and debates set out above that the SSR agenda was born. Having widened the meanings of both 'security sector' and 'reform', what was now required was a means of moulding them into a conceptually presentable package.[17] The term 'security sector reform' was seen to encapsulate this new logic in a single, convenient phrase. This is reflected in the promotion and use of the concept by numerous research and policy-development institutions.

According to International Alert: 'Whilst in the past bilateral security and military assistance was used mainly to promote strategic interests aimed at fostering stability, the donor community has in recent years begun to see what has been termed "security sector reform" as an *explicit development objective*.'[18] International Alert seeks to promote SSR as a key conflict prevention policy and contribute to SSR policy development and implementation. For the Deutsche Gesellschaft für Technische Zusammenarbeit (GTZ) SSR 'embraces not only security from external threat, but also material, physical and social security as well as protection from bodily harm ... *Above all* security sector reform means guaranteeing human security.'[19] Departments within the UN and World Bank began to consider how they could become part of this new agenda. There was an explosion in SSR conferences and seminars. Suddenly, but conveniently, SSR meant everything for everyone. Packaged so neatly, it was easy to present, attracting not only attention, but also considerable material support.

In 1998 Nicole Ball recommended that the British government should 'develop a comprehensive framework for SSR' which would 'integrate issues pertaining to internal security such as policing, administration of justice, and rule of law, with issues relating to the armed forces, the intelligence services, paramilitary forces, and the civilian institutions responsible for managing and monitoring them.' Accordingly, 'The British government should seek to put SSR on the agenda in all relevant multilateral institutions ... All relevant British government ministries and departments should accord top priority to shaping their staffs and providing the necessary resources so that personnel can effectively promote SSR.'[20]

The EU's Conflict Prevention Network invited Saferworld to undertake an assessment of current trends in SSR among its donors.[21] Saferworld's report, written by Malcolm Chalmers and published in January 2000, comprised an impressive list of activities in which the EU was already involved, apparently falling under the rubric of SSR. According to Saferworld's report on the prevention of violent conflict and the coherence of EU policies towards the Horn of Africa published later that year: 'The EU needs to develop a coherent policy on SSR … SSR should be recognized as an integral aspect of democratization and government reform. The EU needs to ensure that there is sufficient financial support to implement SSR … The EU must strengthen institutional expertise on SSR … .'[22]

The main dimensions of the SSR agenda are set out below.

Main Dimensions

The SSR agenda can be divided into four key dimensions: political, institutional, economic and societal. The political dimension of the SSR agenda sets the overall context for SSR; the institutional dimension describes the characteristics of the security sector to which SSR aspires; and the economic and societal dimensions set forth the necessary support mechanisms for successful reform.

The Political Dimension

The political dimension of the SSR agenda determines the character of the management of the security sector. It promotes not only civilian governance, but liberal, democratic civilian control. According to the Department for International Development: 'interest is in helping to secure a security sector of appropriate scale that is properly accountable to democratic, civilian authorities.'[23] According to the GTZ, '*above all* [SSR] includes the civil authorities mandated to control and oversee [security] agencies … Security sector reform is part of a governance reform programme.'[24] According to the 2000 DAC report of the OECD, SSR is understood in terms of 'the transformation of this sector so that it is managed and operates in a manner that is more consistent with democratic norms and sound principles of governance.' The report views SSR as 'fundamentally a question of governance and ... essentially driven by domestic, social and political change.'[25]

The political context that the SSR agenda envisages thus requires a democratically elected government with the ability to exercise control and oversight of the security sector. In order to enforce that control, it typically seeks to establish, *inter alia*, civilian expertise and control in the ministries of defence, justice and internal affairs, together with independent audit units, independent ombudsman offices and civilian review boards.

SSR is therefore about much more than the internal structure of security forces. It promotes the strengthening of norms in relation to the proper relationship between the security sector and society at large. As Chalmers states:

> at the heart of the SSR project as commonly understood is an acceptance of universal norms. When we talk of 'security sector reform', we typically do not mean just any reform, but specific <u>types</u> of reform that move societies closer to norms that are usually quite explicit.[26]

The Institutional Dimension

The security sector itself encompasses all state institutions that have a formal mandate to ensure the safety of the state and its citizens against acts of violence and coercion. Institutional reform focuses upon building up their capacities in line with the standards assumed appropriate to the democratic political context described above.

Building the capacity of the military forces includes 'right-sizing' – disarmament, demobilisation and reintegration of excess forces, as well as the building up of forces that are deemed insufficient to fulfil their roles. It may also involve professionalisation, in particular their reorientation away from domestic politics towards those tasks for which they are considered most appropriate, such as territorial defence and peace-support activities. Building the capacity of police forces may involve a reorientation of their role from support of the military, or involvement in activities traditionally associated with the military, to more appropriate peacetime policing. Apart from these two parts of the security sector, attention is given increasingly to building the capacity of judicial and penal systems, and working to ensure their political independence and accountability through training and support to judges, lawyers, human rights activists and other NGO representatives. Other parts of the security sector that fall within the remit of SSR include the emergency services, border guards, customs and immigration officials, and intelligence services.

The Economic Dimension

The economic dimension of the SSR agenda is concerned with the consumption of resources for the security forces, and revenue collection mechanisms. The provision of clearly accounted defence budgets is a key aspect of the SSR approach to reform, as is the ability to meet the resource demands of an appropriately sized and equipped security sector.

The Societal Dimension

The social dimension of SSR gives an important role to civil society. Community NGOs, independent media, and independent research and advocacy institutions are seen as having important roles to play in monitoring the security sector and ensuring transparency, thereby providing the checks and balances that are necessary for the promotion of democratic control of the security sector.

The State of the Security Sector Reform Debate

The increasing focus of development agencies on security governance issues created the space within which a strategic emphasis on SSR began to emerge. The SSR agenda itself is impressive. It encompasses a diverse array of security institutions, their character, management and control. It also promises a great deal – truly sustainable peace and development. However, its institutional implementation has so far lagged well behind the vision. In many World Bank country sections SSR is not actually being addressed as a core theme. Within the UN, EU and NATO there is no explicit SSR programme, but efforts are rather being made to include existing programmes and projects under this heading.

This lack of institutional planning is accompanied by continuing problems in relating proposed normative changes to the realities of specific contexts. While SSR concepts may sound impressive, and often form the bases of stated donor goals, the success of SSR policy depends on its ability to engage with the local security context operationally. Yet the SSR debate often appears to underplay some of the key problems involved in translating principles into reality. How can values be transferred? How can they be integrated and sequenced and made relevant to specific contexts? What are the minimum requirements for external involvement? The consequences of the lack of attention to these crucial aspects of reform are discussed in the next section.

Chapter 2

Operationalising Security Sector Reform

Implementing SSR

Despite the cogency with which the SSR agenda is presented, operational success has so far occurred, or appears to be occurring, only in relatively exceptional circumstances. In the majority of cases – especially those where the political will or consensus for reform is absent – reform has had at best a limited impact. While new security structures are established to resemble more formal, 'acceptable' security and state institutions, personal, informal security networks continue to flourish and may even become more politically and economically viable at the expense of reform efforts. Examples include Cambodia, Nigeria, Bosnia and Ukraine. Despite reform attempts, violence and instability continue, deepen or re-emerge, such as in El Salvador, Côte d'Ivoire, Palestine and Angola. Security sectors remain in limbo, held together by international actors, and unable to move forward independently, as in Sierra Leone or Kosovo. Insecurity, both for the majority of the state's inhabitants and sometimes also with regard to a state's borders, persists.

The present chapter explores why the visions encompassed in the SSR agenda have had only very limited success operationally. The challenges that reformers face will be discussed in relation to the four dimensions that make up the SSR agenda – political, institutional, economic and societal – and the operationalisation of the agenda itself. The specific problems that arise in terms of the structures, behaviours and institutional characteristics of target countries demonstrate that the way in which the SSR agenda is currently implemented is often no match for the local rationalisation or capacity of security that it seeks to influence. This demonstration points to the need to rethink or begin to think about how SSR can be introduced into reform contexts more effectively, and which specific approaches can be used to overcome the structural and normative realities reformers currently face.

The Political Context: Security Governance in Disputed States

The political dimension of the SSR agenda provides the necessary context or framework for the other elements of reform to occur. However, as attempts to mobilise reform projects in many contexts have illustrated, the elements of good governance and democratic control described in Chapter 1 rest upon certain preconditions. Foremost among these are agreement about the legitimacy of those governing a reform context and their ability to cooperate with each other and internationally; and strategic priorities that privilege citizen security.

Political Legitimacy

The contexts within which SSR has been most successful to date tend to be characterised by at least a semblance of state legitimacy. That is, the presence of democratically elected officials who can cooperate, discuss and reach agreement about the direction of reform of their security sectors, not only among themselves, but also regionally and internationally. However, in many reform contexts the question of political legitimacy is still under negotiation.

In the most extreme cases, as for example in Kosovo, international actors are temporarily invested with legitimacy in order to maintain and reform law and order. Security Council Resolution 1244 of 10 June 1999 vested in UNMIK all legislative and executive powers as well as the administration of the judiciary. The UN Interim Administration Mission in Kosovo is responsible for promoting the establishment of substantial autonomy and self-government in Kosovo, performing basic civil administration functions and facilitating the political process to determine Kosovo's future status, and maintaining law and order and promoting human rights. Key activities include the development of law enforcement institutions in Kosovo, establishing new judicial and penal systems, and developing a Kosovo Police Service following the withdrawal of Serbian Interior Ministry Police according to the NATO-FRY Military Technical Agreement. While the implementation of these activities is severely hampered by ethnic tensions, the authority invested in the international administration at least allows for decision-making about the future shape of the SSR to occur. The major question remains, however, as to how authority can be successfully transferred to indigenous political parties in the long term.

In other post-conflict situations, disputes over political legitimacy make such a process fraught from the outset. Bosnia is a prime example. The Dayton Peace Agreement (DPA) presented still more fundamental challenges to potential security reform. As Tanner explains: 'The DPA legitimised the military partition of the country and its ambiguous language allows the various nationalist parties to pursue their policies of segregation.'[1] While the DPA aimed to achieve a stable military relationship among former belligerents, it did not provide a road map towards security governance. Indeed the compromises required to reach any agreement at all purposefully avoided dealing with the question of political legitimacy. Consequently, external efforts to achieve SSR suffer on a daily basis. The spending of large amounts of international aid on physical reconstruction may have been an immediate priority on humanitarian grounds, but has brought few long-term security benefits. As Marcus Cox points out, in Bosnia, reconstruction assistance disbursed in haste at the local level tended to reinforce parallel power structures, at the expense of the state the international community was trying to maintain.[2]

Bosnia still lacks a national identity and is often characterised by a hostile competition driven by divisive nationalistic and ethnic-oriented priorities. The same kind of division also holds for the police, armed forces, intelligence and judicial system; a lack of consensus and cooperation at the level of governance has severe implications for the overall character of the security sector. As Tanner states: 'in other words, for the time being, the national security sector is dysfunctional and its institutions are missing for the most part.'[3] Until there is a change in the character and attitude of Bosnia's government, and despite the vast sums of money that Western donors have poured into assistance, these external efforts in the economic, institutional and social dimensions of SSR are unlikely to prove fruitful.

Further challenges arise when legitimacy also has to be established regionally and internationally. While the EU and other bilateral donors are providing funding and advice about the reform and creation of a security sector suitable for a Palestinian state, those governing the current security forces in Palestine are still fighting to achieve statehood and recognition. UN involvement in efforts to create a security sector in East Timor are complicated by challenges to both its internal and external legitimacy. Indonesia's armed forces, the TNI, or at least some hardline elements within it, have yet to accept defeat. Militias, who were armed mainly with pipe guns and machetes, have obtained automatic rifles and hand grenades and have received training in guerrilla tactics. The only way that East Timor can survive, military experts say, is if the UN's mandate is extended in a supportive role, or if it reaches bilateral defence agreements with countries such as Australia and New Zealand. A further problem is that the force that was to become East Timor's own army, the armed forces for the liberation of East Timor, FALINTIL, is in total disarray, with breakaway elements undermining efforts to build up a cohesive security sector. It is also not within the UN's mandate to turn the FALINTIL into a more professional force.[4]

The cases targeted for reform are therefore not states in the traditional sense, but quasi-states, virtual states, states in formation and in the process of negotiation. What unites all of the above examples, and most states targeted for reform, is that they are in some way and to various extents disputed. The consequences of these disputes manifest themselves in security sectors whose strategic priorities are quite different from those of the democratic states used as models in the SSR agenda.

Strategic Priorities

Strategic priorities are the primary factors that influence the decisions about security made by those governing the state, or controlling a semblance of 'formal' security apparatus. According to the vision of the SSR agenda the state has a responsibility not only to protect its borders, but foremost to protect its citizens. However, given the disputed character of the states in question, this cannot be taken for granted and can be very difficult to achieve. A reform context may be heavily constrained by what the elite or certain groups of the society with the power to give or take away security identify as being threatening.

Living in a troubled region has had severe consequences for the character of internal state security provisions in much of the Caucasus. During the active period of Georgia's three civil wars, bandit gangs, most notably the *Mkhedrioni* (horsemen), dramatically consolidated support for challengers to the country's territorial integrity or its authority structures. From 1995 onwards quasi-criminal paramilitary groups have emerged once again as important players in western Georgia and as a significant complicating factor in the effort to assure the stability of the Abkhaz–Georgian cease-fire. MacFarlane argues that being surrounded by potentially hostile neighbours enhances the insecurity of the leadership and inhibits any surrender of control over forceful instruments of policy. Hence, the first step to the maintenance of territorial security is political or regime security.[5] And, because of the disputed nature of these states, this is rarely based upon electoral campaigns followed by free and fair elections.

In disputed states the maintenance of political security is therefore also a primary security concern. At times of reform and potential or actual shifts in the nature of security apparatus control, the desire to build up security coalitions and balance potential threats becomes particularly acute for those in newly established or negotiated seats of power. The constraints placed upon reform of security as a consequence of these factors are clearly visible in the Balkans.

In the euphoric mood that followed the installation of the new regime in Serbia in October 2000, neither the Serbian public nor the international community initially noticed that, apart from replacing Slobodan Milosevic and a small band of his immediate associates, very few changes were being made within Milosevic's old security apparatus. Deals between the Democratic Opposition of Serbia and the security organisations to ensure a relatively peaceful transition of power seriously hinder external efforts to undertake significant security reforms within Serbia. Kostunica managed to win the support of the Yugoslav Army only by allowing senior commanders to retain their posts, despite their pro-Milosevic history and activities. Commanding officers and politicians reached a tacit agreement whereby both sides would ignore troublesome issues that would damage their relations and the overall political situation.[6] Kostunica himself commented that the hasty removal of General Markovic and other top figures would work counter to democratic change as it 'runs counter to state interests since it inevitably leads to destabilisation.'[7] This may be true, but it is not a promising starting point for the SSR agenda.

In disputed states the ideal of investing what there is of state capacity in citizen security remains just that – an ideal. Alternative and more immediate security governance priorities circumscribe the potential and will for change, or at least influence its direction away from the security of individuals within the state's borders to both the maintenance of those borders and an uncompromising control of the political and security apparatus necessary to undertake such maintenance. The implications of these pressures for the institutional character of these states' security sectors are far-reaching.

Institutional Characteristics: Diversity and Tradition in Security Forces

As the SSR agenda illustrates, external reformers frequently emphasise the importance of the institutional characteristics that they wish to imbue in the security forces of reform contexts. This may be in terms of functional differentiation, identity, doctrine or professionalisation. Most often it involves drawing clear boundaries between those forces responsible for maintaining internal control and those responsible for the defence of a state's borders; between those responsible for bringing a resolution to conflict and those responsible for its continuation. However, the institutional characteristics already present in the recipients' societies are also of vital importance and play a key role both in shaping security traditions and imbuing security sectors with an identity and purpose. These alternative identities and traditions present security sector reformers with particular behavioural and structural problems when it comes to implementing reform efforts.

Constitutional Diversity – The Functions of the Security Forces

Many of the cases targeted for reform have constitutions that mandate that their militaries play significantly different roles to those portrayed in the ideal type. In other cases, although no official constitutional arrangements may exist, the security sector is accepted as being a much more fluid entity, characterised by the militarisation of public security functions and politics more generally, and an absence of a clear distinction between the spheres of the military and police – often seen to be a clear precondition of the SSR agenda.

The role of the Indonesian Armed Forces (TNI) is an example of the former. The TNI has been interwoven in Indonesia's political landscape since the beginning of the country's independence in 1949. As a key player in securing Indonesia's independence, the TNI has historically seen itself as more than a military institution. The TNI-codified concept of *dwifungsi* or dual function, evolves from the military's perception that it is rightfully both a political and military institution. *Dwifungsi* is an assertion that it is legitimate and necessary for the Indonesian armed forces to take on both military and non-military roles. In its traditional role, the military's responsibility is to ensure the defence and security of the republic; in its non-military role, the armed forces are a political entity that function as the guardian of the people and can control appointments to important civil service and governmental positions. The *dwifungsi* concept was endorsed as a doctrine for the armed forces in 1966 and given constitutional standing when it was passed as state law in 1982.[8] The doctrine itself has been discarded, but its replacement, *peran TNI* – TNI role – is essentially a modernised version of the same concept. There has been no urgency on the TNI's part to discard its territorial doctrine, under which the military command structure shadows the civilian administration down to the village level, often in an oppressive manner. Even with the installation of President Megawati Sukarnoputri on 23 July 2001, the role of the military is still of paramount import-ance – this time not as the force that underpinned the 32 years of autocratic rule of former President Suharto, but as the supporter of a democracy that refused to implement the emergency one-man rule sought by Wahid.[9] Marrying these traditions with the objec-tives of the SSR agenda is proving a major challenge for external reformers operating in Indonesia, such as USAID and DFID.

The military establishments in much of Africa are perhaps the most fluid. The character of many African security sectors is such that it is hard to distinguish between the roles of the main players. Internal security, traditionally under the police and law enforcement agencies, has become the function of a mixture of forces: the national army, police and various security agencies including paramilitaries and the presidential guards. Most African police are paramilitary, while the military usually take over aspects of basic enforcement in the extreme circumstances to be found in much of the continent.[10] For example the late President Mobutu Sese Seko's strategy to survive mounting political opposition was to fragment the security and armed forces when it became imposs-ible to ensure their loyalty. While the army was allowed to dwin-dle in size, a succession of clandestine special strike forces was formed, deployed and then dissolved.[11]

Western norms of policing are no more readily transportable than those of the military. The Palestinian security forces were initially formed with Israel's consent and were designed to create an active and strong police presence to prevent 'terrorism', provide for Israeli security, and counter internal strife in the West Bank and Gaza. However, following the outbreak of the intifada in October 2000, a major question regarding the development of Palestinian military capabilities is whether these forces are shifting their inten-tions from the provisions of the 1994 Cairo Agreement with Israel, towards the formation of a rudimentary army primarily concerned with defending Palestinian borders. Efforts to implement the security sector reforms recommended by the EU or other bilateral donors clearly take second place to the imperatives of everyday survival.

In other reform contexts, not only do the police see the public as the enemy rather than someone they are working to assist, but the public, or certain sections of it, also see the police as a body to fear, rather than trust. In Kosovo, the totally Serbian-dominated Yugoslav police, and in particular the special police, MUP, were much more oriented towards controlling the local population than serving them. The training being coordinated under the auspices of UNMIK, UN Civilian Police (CIVPOL) and International Criminal Investigative Training Assistance Program (ICITAP) is grounded in human rights education, but whether or not such education is sufficient to overcome the aftermath of the civil conflict in the area remains to be seen.

Writing about the identity of the Haitian police force, its militaristic tendencies and lack of a social security ethos, Joseph Trincellito, Chief of Planning and Evaluation, ICITAP, argues that the concept of civilian policing – serving the needs of the public – 'is not well understood either by the Haitian armed forces nor by much of the populace'.[12] Trincellito's explanation is, however, questionable. Rather than not being understood, it may be that the concepts do not fulfil a 'useful' role in the local security contexts in which they are employed. External attempts to reshape the security forces of these states have proved extremely problematic, which suggests that SSR is about much more than simply overcoming misunderstandings. The blurring of boundaries between such a multiplicity of functions can serve quite specific purposes, as can the ability to mobilise and demobilise according to particular situations. For those who hold the reins of power these arrangements represent the best means of maintaining that power. There is therefore great reluctance to change such arrangements, or a will only to change them very superficially. This perspective is given added credence in view of the fact that, even as reform measures are implemented, these alternative security identities find ways of re-establishing or maintaining their presence and control.

Re-inventing Tradition

While the structure of security institutions may change as a consequence of reform efforts, experience has illustrated that the attitudes beneath them may remain deeply wedded to tradition. In

Latin America the end of military rule did not abolish the prerogatives and self-appointed role of the armed forces to deal with threats. Violent backlashes in response to social mobilisation or upheavals remain a common feature of post-authoritarian governance. The military retained substantial control over the formulation of policy in sensitive areas using the intelligence system as their principal vehicle. Despite substantial assistance from the EU, in countries such as Chile, Peru, Guatemala and Brazil, the elected or appointed presidents are the ideological hostages of their intelligence advisors. A further element bequeathed by the militarisation of politics in most Latin American countries – Chile being the exception – is the military predominance over the national and local police. It is still common for army officers to hold sensitive posts in the police hierarchy, and the political responsibility for the national police is often a matter of civil–military power distribution. The inviolability of the officer corps during the anti-guerrilla and anti-narcotics campaigns of the last decades in Colombia, El Salvador, Guatemala and Peru is remembered as a chronic obstacle to reform efforts.[13]

South Africa represents a different example of the consequences of security traditions reinventing themselves. The early police forces in South Africa were largely paramilitary forces that were established to protect the interests of early settlers from the 'threats' posed by indigenous people. The South African Police was founded and developed within the context of racially exclusive power. Under apartheid, these security institutions had little interest in responding to crimes within black areas. Their presence in townships was used to anticipate and diffuse and to provide 'fireforce' responses to collective challenges to apartheid. Such interventions typically involved the targeting of resources for short periods of time in response to resistance by blacks to white rule.[14] Since the end of apartheid much progress has been made with the reform of South Africa's security forces. Locally driven efforts have received much support from Western and international donors. However, a parallel pattern of discrimination is now emerging within the security sector, not this time based on a racial distinction, but on the divisions which exist between the rich and the poor.[15]

Efforts to remove the military from politics in Nigeria also present a mixed record. A military disengagement process, often euphemistically referred to as Transition to Civil Rule Programme, was completed on 29 May 1999 with the handover of power to elected civilian leaders. However, the disengagement process produced the emergence of the 'retired soldier' as a new but very powerful phenomenon in Nigerian politics. Retired soldiers have regrouped to dominate the political space. The military authored the demilitarisation process and became the only actor in its disengagement process. The institutional base of militarism was neither deconstructed nor reformed in the demilitarisation plan. These include the police forces, which under the military regimes acted as a force for terrorising the civil populace, and the state security service (SSS), which was transformed into a mafia group. There was blatant abuse and manipulation of the judiciary and the judicial process, as the issue of appointment, promotion, tenure and security of office of judges depended largely on the whims and caprices of the military rulers. It was not uncommon therefore to see Judges referring to the military rulers as *Kabiyesi* (His Royal Majesty), whose actions or decisions cannot be questioned or inquired into by the citizens. In 2000 it was estimated that no less than 130 rich and influential retired military officers were members of the Peoples Democratic Party (PDP), the ruling party in Nigeria at the Federal Level.[16]

As security sector reformers have discovered and as Adejumobi explains: 'The practice of militarisation is not necessarily synonymous with only military rule, but present also in civil regimes. Post-military states usually have entrenched norms and practices of militarism that are not easily deconstructed or eradicated with the formal transfer of political power from the military to civilians.'[17] Given the fact that these traditions are so durable and resourceful in their reinvention, an exploration of how they maintain themselves structurally, ideologically and materially is key to understanding more fully the security sectors in question.

Alternative Security Mechanisms

As Christopher Clapham has argued in relation to many parts of

Africa, the 'ideal of public security cannot be plausibly achieved.'[18] The security traditions explored above make no such distinction. State and society are not exclusive domains. Formal and informal boundaries are inherently blurred. Security forces are also neither professional nor objective in the traditional sense of the words. Informal security communities exist in which security is not just the preserve of the state but also a whole multiplicity of actors. The state itself has, in certain places, become what Eboe Hutchful has called a 'security racket' in which potential leaders abuse official state power and patronage to provide security to influential societal groups that underpin their position of power.[19] However, it is not just immediately identifiable influential groups in society that are able to afford security. The ideas and relationships connecting and counterbalancing this security racket are rich in their ingenuity and potential inclusiveness. Security is not only to be given or taken; it is also out there to be made.

Kinship and Ethnicity

A common strategy employed by a regime to retain control of security is the manipulation of the bonds of kinship and ethnicity. Members of government or those in key security positions are often recruited from specific tribes or ethnic affiliations favourable to political elites, and are well placed to exploit their coercive abilities, communications and intelligence resources. Further, it is rarely in their interest – or, more importantly, in those of the regime on whose behalf they work – to reform or become efficient or effective. It was not by accident that President Laurent Kabila of the Democratic Republic of the Congo surrounded himself with members of his family and tribesmen, appointing them to top positions in government security agencies and the army. His brother-in-law was chief of the army and his son the deputy.

Even where reform is declared, bloodlines generally run thicker and deeper than democracy. Since the 'democratic' election on 7 January 2001 in Ghana, there have been significant changes in the security sector. In the military the hierarchy of seven top generals was asked to go on leave. However, discussions reported with some serving officers paint a picture of one ethnic group replacing its favourites with another. The politics of ethnicity, which characterised the previous elections, was perceptible in the way in which security-related appointments and decisions are being made. This presents a convenient paradox in many African societies. While African police forces or armed forces are invariably under-resourced, individual officers are well placed to exploit their relationships and knowledge, and security organisations are remarkably tenacious.[20]

These bonds are also key to the provision of security within society more generally. Perhaps the most extreme example of their penetration is seen in the case of Somalia, where both militia and civilian authorities are structured around systems of clans and 'Big Men'. The militia and their 'technicals' – jeeps mounted with heavy weaponry – remain deeply wedded to their respective clans.[21] Outside of the armed elements of Somali society, the clan leadership has undergone a process of 'civilianisation', with the emergence of clan-based civilian authorities performing governance functions.[22] In Palestine, the unofficial clan-based judicial systems date back to the time of the Arab revolt in 1930. In parts of the Balkans, the roles played by clans also remain very important. The clan structure is particularly strong in Kosovo and Northern Albania where, parallel to its utilisation in Palestine, it represents informal political institutions organised by traditional law, rather than the 'official' law.

Inter-communal Associations

Even in the absence of strong clan or kinship traditions, societies and sectors of society find means of 'making' security, or counterbalancing state-sponsored security. These are often based upon inter-communal associations or initiatives taken by sectors of communities that face common security challenges.

One of the most documented cases of 'making' security is that of South Africa. Under apartheid, within black areas, the local governance of security was left to the people themselves. Black South Africans responded by developing a variety of civil structures for governing their own security ranging from vigilante groups, such as People Against Gangsterism and Drugs, to dispute resolution processes at the street and area level. The fact that South

African policing was based on a wide base of civilian involvement and the mobilisation of a wide network of resources was obscured during the entire apartheid period because of the visibility of fireforce policing which came to be seen as emblematic of South African security in general.[23] Although it was given little attention, community policing in South Africa was therefore happening long before the phrase was popular after 1994.

Privatisation

Privatisation of security can be thought of in terms of a more exclusive method of 'security making.' Private security companies are not a new phenomenon, but demand for them has escalated since the early 1990s. After the Cold War, the unravelling of patron–client systems, the increasing reluctance of Western governments to intervene militarily in situations where they do not now have any strategic interest, and the downsizing of numerous armed forces leaving a surplus of semi-retired soldiers, has led to the emergence of new types of 'private' national and international security entrepreneurs. The most extreme manifestation of private security activity has been companies acting as private armies to perform peace-enforcement functions as seen in Angola and Sierra Leone with the use of Executive Outcomes.[24]

The downsizing of armed forces has also led to the proliferation of domestic security companies in many regions including the former Soviet Union, Central America, and Southern Africa. When apartheid officially ended in South Africa some soldiers set up lucrative security firms which supply mercenaries – a system with origins in the ancient world dating back to the Greeks and the Carthaginians – to Angola, Sierra Leone, Congo and Papua-New Guinea.[25]

A Multiplicity of Security Orders

This multiplicity of security orders presents external actors interested in SSR with several challenges. First, there is the challenge of understanding how security actually works in the reform context itself. Secondly, there is the need to convince the state and society targeted for reform of the advantages of reform and perhaps the replacement of traditional methods of security provisions. Thirdly, there are risks that elements of the traditional security sector will either reinvent themselves or compete and undermine new security structures. The inability to overcome these challenges can lead to attempts to impose reform.

Imposition itself ranges from a passive approach to reform that shows little understanding of the local context, to examples whereby external actors seem determined to impose their own way of doing things. For example, as MacFarlane points out, the European reform agenda in Georgia is based upon an individualistic approach and conception of statehood whereas Georgian society is family and horizontally organised and proceeds on the informal linkages of patronage networks. It is therefore questionable as to how durable Georgia's apparent acceptance of European norms will be.[26]

Commentators on the role of the US in Latin America make a similar point, questioning what the US administration means by professionalisation of the armed forces and police of a Latin American country. According to the Washington Office on Latin America (WOLA), 'it means subjection to a policy of the US and of the international financial institutions ... by which the rule of law becomes equivalent to unconditional respect for the law of market forces,' using security forces to repress popular mobilisations that question neo-liberal policies. Ultimately, WOLA argues, this translates into a willingness to violate citizens' human rights.[27]

One of the most extreme examples of imposition is seen in the case of post-Dayton Bosnia. In a speech to the UN Security Council on 8 November 1999, High Commissioner Petritsch explained that legislative imposition was central to the concept of 'Ownership'. He stated: 'imposition ... does not run contrary to the concept of Ownership'[28]. Rather it would, 'substantially improve the democratic process in Bosnia.'[29] In 1999, the Office of the High Representative (OHR) imposed 45 decisions as compared to 16 the previous year.[30] Petritsch described such a strategy as being necessary in order to create a 'level playing field' before 'stepping back and letting the players get on with the game.'[31] However, as the lack of progress with reform efforts in Bosnia illustrates, getting on with the game is not so straightforward. Enforcement without some measure of consent – even when it is a possibility – has never produced sustainable change. This is primarily because of a lack of home-grown economic and social support.

Economic Support: Shadow Networks and 'Acceptable' Corruption

The SSR agenda calls for the introduction of effective accounting, financing and budgeting of the security sector in order to support, right-size, train and equip internal and military security forces. However, reform contexts pose two critical challenges. First, the budgets of states targeted for reform are generally in poor shape. For example, the capacity of the Georgian budget to carry SSR is low. The process of privatisation of state property has been essentially uncontrolled and highly predatory. In addition, the performance of the tax authorities in effectively collecting revenue has been disappointing. To a certain extent external aid can help to correct this problem by providing financial support to institutional building. However, the second and more fundamental challenge to effecting and sustaining the economic supports for which the SSR agenda calls is the fact that both state and society are riven by corruption.

Corruption cross-cuts and in some cases unites the diversity of security traditions described above. It requires that state actors make use of non-state, unofficial channels, that foes become friends, and that ideological and structural differences are set aside, at least momentarily. These remarkably fluid and convenient connections are referred to as shadow networks: groups of people acting below, above and within the state to improve their material and political standing on the basis of economic or other material linkages. The effects of the workings of these networks upon attempts to sustain SSR efforts can be explored on three levels: official, societal, and regional or international.

Official Corruption

Officials in disputed states often depend upon their ability to raise funds through shadow networks in order to maintain themselves and the status quo. Examples are numerous. Sierra Leone's army has a history of pursuing private profit, a trend that UK SSR assistance aims to redress. According to MacFarlane, 'money and power in Georgia are interchangeable', while in the Ukraine, as Sherr explains, there is a desire for reform, 'but this will go as far as personal or corporate interests and then stop ...'[32] In Cambodia, the military structures that do function are to a large degree made possible by profitable commercial activities rather than public resources or a state-led security strategy. In the past, Indonesia's armed forces have also relied on non-budgetary income from extensive commercial operations, as well as extortion and corruption, with the official defence budget meeting only a fraction of their needs. The spectre of KKN (*Korupsu Konclusi Nepotisma*) is still present.

The consequences of official corruption are well illustrated in the case of Nigeria. In Nigeria, appointment to, promotion within and funding of all state institutions is determined largely by networks of personal and informal connections with the leadership in conjunction with heavily corrupted, unaudited accounts. The consequence is that public institutions have became thoroughly depreciated and devalued and cannot deliver public goods and services effectively or guarantee public welfare. For example, the police force, rather than protect the people, has often terrorised them for its own profits, the civil service, rather than facilitate government business, has became privatised through a culture of bribery and corruption, and public services like electricity, water supply and telecommunications have virtually collapsed.[33]

Official corruption has been a major impediment to the socio-economic and political advancement of Ghana since independence. Its pervasive influence on public decision-making processes has been both cause and consequence of structural and economic decay. A recent diagnostic study of the problem showed a strong culture of graft in several government institutions. Some of the institutions that rated low in terms of honesty and integrity were the police, government ministers, political parties, the customs and excise, the judiciary, the Ministry of Finance and the Lands Commission.[34]

The extent of official corruption in the Balkans is also striking. The arrest in August 2000 of Alija Delimustafic, a Party of Democratic Action stalwart, one of Bosnia's top bankers and interior minister when the Bosnian war began in 1992, is but one example. The Delimustafic case, implicating leading SDA politicians in the theft of some US$15 million in Western Aid, showed how deep the shadow networks in Sarajevo ran. Worse still was the scandal that broke in early November 2000 around Bosnian Prime Minister Edhem Bicakcic. Bicakcic, another SDA veteran stands accused of defrauding Bosnian taxpayers of tens of millions of dollars through a network of private, SDA-concerned companies.[35]

The legacies of the problems resulting from the deep involvement of elements within the security organisations in Milosevic's regime of unlimited personal rule and state-sanctioned crime look set to remain for many years to come. The tenacity of the old guard to remain intact is both a consequence of and reflected in the presence and continuation of shadow networks. According to Zoran Kusovac, there is hardly a genuine desire to eradicate Serbian police crime, but instead an attempt to bring it under control of new masters and perhaps to avoid some of the excesses.[36] However, it is not only state officials that are corrupt and important players in shadow networks – societies themselves have a key role to play.

Shadows in Society

Shadow networks depend upon maintaining connections within society. Due to the extent of external involvement, Bosnian society provides a particularly vivid example of shadow activity. SFOR's nation-building campaign has not been without successes, but considering the cost – at least US$5 billion in humanitarian aid – many Westerners and Bosnians alike have begun to wonder what the West has really achieved for such an overwhelming expenditure in a country of only 4 million people. Rampant corruption lies at the heart of Bosnia. In both Bosnian entities widespread theft by governments entrenched in society by their mafia affiliates has become routine.

The relations between organised crime syndicates and political leaders in Bosnia are a prominent characteristic of the Bosnian security landscape. The proceeds from the narcotics trade are widely believed to support illegal institutions maintained by ethnic extremists. Criminal leaders are ready to threaten judges, prosecutors, police officers, lawyers, or witnesses with violence, even death, to act in a particular way.[37] Attempts to reform Bosnia's criminal justice system have been severely hampered by such threats. In a poll taken in November 2000, Bosnians listed the intertwined issues of economic hardship and corruption as their top concerns, for the first time placing ethnic issues far behind, in fourth place. The effects of these networks and their dependencies extend not only inwards towards society, but also outwards across state and international boundaries.

Regional and International Consequences

Again the Balkans provides a vivid example. Post-revolution events have shown that Serbia's uniformed police were involved with a vast array of shady deals with mafias across the region, regardless of their ethnic allegiance. The role of the Public Security Department of the Serbian Ministry for the Interior, the *Resor javne bezbednosti* (RJB), in the highly lucrative transnational cigarette trade was a major fundraiser for Public Security. The involvement of the Ministry for the Interior in the drugs trade was also long suspected by regime critics. Belgrade's prominent position on the Balkan heroin route dates back to the 1960s. How deeply the RJB was involved in drug smuggling became evident on 3 October 2000, only two days before the fall of Milosevic, when Venezuelan officials seized 38 kg of cocaine hidden among the possession of Milosav Markovic, the police attaché at the Yugoslav Embassy in Caracas.[38]

In some cases, the involvement of the international community also provides a space within which shadow networks flourish. Economic reform initiatives offer further opportunities for enterprising networkers. Despite the original intention of Structural Adjustment Programmes to allow the market to be emancipated from the clutches of the state in Africa, they have served to buttress the position of the elite since they have delivered huge financial resources into their hands. Increasing numbers of politicians are heavily involved in illicit financial and commercial transactions – from money laundering to drug smuggling. According to the *African Security Review*, Africa is not thus simply a victim of globalisation. Rather, its elites are active participants in the informal world market, 'the underside of the globalised economy that appears to be passing by the continent'. For those that are now thriving on the global informal economy and their clients, enrichment without development is a most profitable situation.[39] The consequences of these transactions for the possibility both of international regulation and of domestic accountability are important. Returning to the initial security problematic presented at the start of this chapter, they represent key disincentives for building up or maintaining a centralised state capacity.

The UN-sanctioned arms and oil embargoes that were imposed on the former Yugoslavia from 1992 onwards created an ideal environment for organised crime syndicates who specialised in smuggling restricted products (as well as many other kinds of merchandise) into Yugoslavia. The smugglers frequently cooperated with government officials and several key political leaders benefited extensively from these activities. Albania and Kosovo are today major points of transit for the smuggling of drugs and illegal immigrants into Central and Western Europe. The syndicates use threats and violence extensively in order to expand, and they are very difficult to infiltrate and fight owing to strong family and clan bonds.[40]

Social Support: Uncivil Society

In liberal civil society theory, as with much of the SSR agenda, civil society is believed to be the most effective agency of democratising society and the best antidote to military or authoritarian rule. Just as effective SSR requires a capable state, so too it relies upon the existence of functioning civic institutions. The Deutsche Gesellschaft für Technische Zusammenarbeit (GTZ) goes so far as to recommend to potential security sector reformers that: 'In case of doubt … cooperation for reform take place primarily with civil society, instead of embarking on questionable programmes with the immediate actors of the security sector, the consequences of which cannot be foreseen.'[41] The privileged position attributed to civil society within GTZ's statement, however, overlooks the potential problems which may often characterise civil society itself.

State Control

One of the first hurdles faced by security sector reformers seeking to involve civil society is the invasiveness of the state. The 'civil-ness' of a society may be virtually non-existent in the traditional Weberian sense. In the Ukraine, as Sherr points out, traditions of security are unlike those of the West. Security sectors are instruments of control of civil society. At the same time, the state guards access to so-called civic institutions jealously.[42]

According to Huxley, there is little incentive for South-east Asian governments to increase the transparency of their security sectors. In general, national defence establishments in the region view the notion of transparency negatively, because of its potential to reveal both their weaknesses, which might tempt aggression, and their strengths, which might stimulate counter-measures. These attitudes have influenced the character of 'national research institutes'. In most South-east Asian countries, these are either extensions of national government bureaucracies or are financially dependent on government ministries or the armed forces. Official nominees and representatives of these think tanks have dominated South-east Asian participation in the supposedly non-official AS-EAN Regional Forum (ARF) 'second track' activities, together with the related Council for Security Cooperation in the Asia-Pacific process.[43] Similar patterns are to be found in many parts of the Middle East, Africa and Latin America.

A Divided Society

A further challenge to the privileged role of civil society is the question of the cohesiveness of the society itself. In both Angola and Sierra Leone, a key issue identified as blocking progress to SSR is the warring parties' lack of trust or willingness to embark on a programme of national reconciliation. Setting state invasiveness to one side, there may be no single 'society' to deal with, but deeply divided groups whose very objectives act to prevent its formation. Writing with the case of South Africa in mind a local security think-tank explains: 'It is important to bear in mind that civil society is composed of many diverse elements, and is divided between supporters of different and opposed social and political courses of action. It is not inherently egalitarian but rather a reflection of the divisions that exist in society itself ... .'[44]

These remarks are equally valid when one considers the Balkans. For example, as discussed with reference to the political dimension of reform, reform in Bosnia is conditioned and limited by the efforts to create a stable deterrence relationship between the Muslim-Croat Federation and the Republic of Srpska. There is little or no dialogue and exchange between the security sector con-stituents of the three ethnic groups. Not surprisingly, this exclu-sionary mentality is replicated socially and continues to define threat assessments in Bosnia today: the main enemy is still internal and it may be geographically very close to home.[45]

A Tyrannical Society

Where social capacity does exist it may be far from democratic. In Nigeria, civil society is plagued by severe contradictions some of which could be considered as part of the backlash of long years of military rule. Many Nigerian civil society groups, especially hu-man rights and pro-democracy groups, lack internal accountability and responsiveness. Some leaders of these groups could be best described as 'small tyrants' who run their organisations like per-sonal fiefdoms. According to Said Adejumobi, they have inter-nalised the signs, symbols and behaviour of military leaders. There is also a culture of opportunism and financial aggrandisement, due to incentives from external funding. Thus there has been the rise of a crop of civil society entrepreneurs, to whom NGO activity is a business enterprise through which they make profit and illegally accumulate wealth. Some civil society groups continue to use the tactics of force and violence as a method and language of political expression, rather than dialogue, negotiation and consensus.[46] This makes it virtually impossible to build a critical consensus about how to take action and how to enter into dialogue with the state about security change.

Lack of Civic Capacity

The civil society qualities and civic institutions that could support SSR efforts may thus be absent from the majority of reform examples. For example, in El Salvador, Honduras, Guatemala and Nicaragua, despite growing public support for police reform and considerable Western donor assistance, specific security reform proposals are lacking. Public discussion remains at a superficial level, with few informed actors in the debate. In El Salvador, according to Guido Bejar, sectors of civil society – including NGOs – have not fully adjusted to the new post-conflict situation. He noted a history of *denuncia,* or denouncing, of government policies and abuses, but little experience in offering proposals for modifying those policies or practices.[47] The lack of public understanding is of particular concern in cases such as that of Guatemala, where peace negotiations take policy issues into account and popular support for reform is critical.[48]

Civil society therefore cannot be a 'magic bullet' which injects good practice. When this lack of support mechanisms for reform within the economy and societies of reform targets is seen in relation to the lack of coherence that has characterised SSR implementation to date, the holistic vision that drives the SSR agenda seems even further out of reach.

Operational Coherence: Institutional and Donor Interests

The lynchpin of the SSR agenda is the fact that it claims to be an integrated approach: it is set apart from previous external involvement in the security sectors of states because of the breadth of its concerns and prescriptions. However, quite apart from the challenges that are to be found in contexts targeted for reform, donors often bring with them their own set of concerns that can seriously jeopardise the agenda's holistic vision.

Motivating Factors

The proposals generated as a result of the SSR agenda typically overlook the interests of the donors themselves. At the very general level of the SSR agenda, the motivations of donors are cohesive and uncontroversial. The holistic approach seems relatively unproblematic. However, it is when SSR is contextualised that difficulties begin to arise. At this more specific level, international assistance to armed forces, police and other law enforcement agencies may often be guided, and constrained, more by the commercial and political interests of donor governments than by an overriding commitment to promoting sustained development through improving security.

This perspective helps to explain why the geographical absence of donor support for reform can be as revealing as its presence. There is little priority given to reform proposals when these might threaten major arms markets or undermine close military allies. Leading Western states, for example, give little time or effort to arguing for greater democratic accountability and transparency for the Gulf armed forces. There is also, at the very least, some tension for major arms exporting states when South African procurement decisions come under increased internal scrutiny.

Moreover, external assistance to security sectors is still often shaped by factors that predate the emergence of the new SSR agenda in the 1990s. One of the most high-profile examples of external support for SSR at the present time is Colombia, where massive external resources, mainly from the US, but also the EU, are being devoted to 'Plan Colombia.' In this case, outside intervention is shaped most of all by a drugs strategy reliant on military containment that is deeply controversial, within and outside Colombia itself.

Cooperation versus Fragmentation

Further fragmentation is apparent within international and regional institutions. UNDP's involvement in police reform remains controversial for many UN member states, which perceive this as an undue violation of sovereignty. Some people within the UNDP also feel that the organisation should focus on more conventional development activities. Consequently, the UNDP's efforts in this field have been an ad hoc process by which candidates for reform have been selected, funding provided and programmes designed.[49] Other documented examples demonstrate similar inconsistencies within the European approaches to reform. EC Directorate VIII, responsible for channelling development assistance to Africa, the Caribbean and the Pacific, contains no mechanism to link assistance to improvements in democracy and human rights, despite espoused SSR objectives. Likewise, the EU takes a project-based approach, focusing primarily on the provision of technical assistance or financing, with much less emphasis placed on using political pressure to affect the policy environment.[50] All SSR operations to date are highly decentralised and there has been little review of lessons learned about what works and what does not.

Fragmentation may also occur within national approaches to SSR. The UK's Strategic Defence Review implies that other government departments will have to accommodate the MoD's new SSR approach, but it is not clear how military forces will interact with the other policy instruments normally used for conflict prevention or resolution. Hills concludes that 'Such a policy is more likely to result in interdepartmental conflict than efficient cooperation,' with 'battles for resources between the departments most concerned.'[51] Despite the apparently consensual rhetoric that glosses the SSR package, reform itself is deeply politicised from the outset. The consequences are felt operationally.

Disagreements about the motivations and specific objectives of reform in the Balkans are manifested in the character of the institutional response. The High Representative, Ambassador Klein, claims that since 1995 the 'international community' has lacked strategic vision and that the external actors were working on the basis of a dysfunctional organisational structure with five organisations more often duplicating than complementing each other. For example, the US's continuous support of the Train and Equip programme encounters European scepticism and outright opposition. The different views are then articulated via the OHR in Bosnia and Herzegovina, the OSCE, its mission in Bosnia and the personal representative of the Chairman in Office of the OSCE.

The lack of coherence between international economic policy and that of other international actors has also proved problematic.

For example, the IMF and World Bank are driving direct involvement with military reform programmes in Cambodia. Yet their immediate priorities conflict with the wider goals of SSR and rehabilitation that UNTAC was responsible for co-ordinating. In a bid to reduce military expenditure rapidly, they adopted a downsizing strategy in 1999. This was based on a combination of conditionalities and support for demobilisation. However, demobilisation efforts foundered due to a lack of government commitment and poor management. The narrow focus on downsizing the armed forces and reducing military spending deflected attention from Cambodia's internal security needs, particularly in the rural areas where most of the country's poor population lives. To give another example, in order to keep within the IMF spending limits, El Salvador was unable to afford building a national civil police force and embarking on arms-for-land programmes to reintegrate guerrillas as required by the peace agreement.[52]

Underlying these shortfalls in the framing of reform operationally is a desire on the part of those concerned to manage risk and to control the environment within which they are operating. There is a tendency to portray reform goals as tangible in order to gain financial support for projects, and to make them fail-safe by setting boundaries that can be moved.

Policy Inconsistencies

The Stability Pact for southeastern Europe is one example of the inconsistencies that hound reform efforts. The Pact was initiated largely as a consequence of the recognition of the importance of implementing security changes in the region. However, the least developed of the three working groups is that concerned with security. Of the relatively small number of security-related projects that have been identified and funded, the majority of funds are allotted for demining. In addition there is no regional strategy. Woodward offers three levels of explanation for this paradox. At the institutional level, the EU is not a security organisation, or at least it is new to the field, while the international financial institutions are legally prohibited from being engaged in security. The

second explanation is that there is insufficient knowledge of security issues. While there is a vague sense that the general climate
is one of insecurity there are few specifics and the divide between
military and civilian matters continues to dominate scholars as well
as practitioners. The third explanation is duplicity. According to
Woodward: 'We say that insecurity is the greatest problem, but we
may not really believe it. If one looks at the theories underlying
assistance policies to the region, security is absent. Donors argue
that political institutions must be created, and they will provide the
conditions for economic growth ... [but] security simply does not
occur in our understanding of transition.'[53]

Certainly, other cases lend resonance to this point. Despite
nearly a decade of experience and indications of the importance of
the judiciary, reformers still pay the issue scant attention. It was six
months before Kosovo's period without the rule of law was settled
on paper. In the end UNMIK brought back into force the Yugoslav
legislation that had existed prior to 1989. It also appointed 400
judges. But the police and the judiciary were not properly
equipped to deal with the everyday reality: undermanned and
lacking in credibility they could not counter the criminality and
control by the mafia who had taken advantage of post-war con-
fusion. With a derisory manning level, the international police –
some 2,500 of the 4,800 expected and the 6,000 requested by
UNMIK – were unable to pursue their investigations very far. They
also came up against a wall of silence and the language barrier.
According to Pekmez, the first waves of local police (the police
college is to train 3,500 at the rate of 250 every two months) are
simply 'a back-up force of little more than symbolic value.' For
more than six months criminals arrested were released due to the
lack of legislation and courts that could send them to prison. More
than 4,000 arrests took place up to January 2000, but only 200
people were actually imprisoned. Once judges were appointed and
the legal framework had been defined, the ethnic question immediately became an issue. Serb defendants objected to Albanian Judges
and vice-versa. Most judges required round-the-clock protection.
Albanian judges were reluctant to prosecute defendants from their
own community for fear of reprisals. The solution to freeing up the
administration of justice was to appoint foreign magistrates.[54]

Conclusion: Infrastructural Dilemmas

The intensely political character of the SSR process is at the heart of all the operational challenges discussed above. The overarching theme running through all of these challenges is that the *infrastructure* – normative as well as structural – the full implementation of SSR objectives requires is usually lacking. While the SSR agenda presents a vision of the end-state of reform, it usually fails to examine how the process of reaching that state can be facilitated in practice. Chapter 3 therefore moves through this process, discussing ways in which these challenges can be approached and presenting concrete policy recommendations for SSR engagement.

Chapter 3

Key Elements for Engagement: Policy Recommendations

Despite the difficulties that external assistance in SSR has encountered to date, it is possible to identify areas and means for implementing specific, concrete reforms that fit in with the overall ethos that the SSR agenda promotes. The areas in question reflect the specific measures that need to be taken in order both to work with the infrastructure of the reform contexts and also that of external reformers themselves. The process of thinking about how and where to engage with reform concretely can be broken down into three policy stages: a pre-implementation stage, the implementation stage itself, and reform consolidation. The pre-implementation stage concentrates on how to make SSR policy planning more effective. The implementation stage focuses upon the points of entry for external actors in reform contexts and the ways in which local ownership of the reform process can be achieved. The consolidation stage is concerned with sustaining and building on reform efforts, and verifying reform progress.

Preparing the Ground: Pre-implementation Considerations
Re-orient Research to Bridge the Conceptual–Contextual Divide

As the discussions that characterise the origins of the SSR agenda illustrate, there is an imbalance in the SSR debate: the concept of SSR is often discussed and written about, but there has been relatively little consideration and investigation of reform contexts.

This research imbalance accounts for the lack of attempts to date to bridge the gaps between the infrastructural characteristics of reform contexts and those of the SSR agenda. While there exist regional experts who can give thorough analyses of the security sectors of states targeted for reform, the relationship between their research and knowledge and SSR concept builders needs to be established in a more systematic fashion that attempts to overcome the conceptual–contextual divide.

Place a Greater Emphasis on Softer Issues of Reform

Within SSR research itself there is a further tendency towards imbalance. While the hard core of technical issues that SSR raises is relatively well-rehearsed and documented, particularly when it comes to military right-sizing, doctrinal presentations, professionalisation drills, budgetary calculations and other similar institutional check-lists, the relationship of these institutions and requirements to society are much less well-understood and receive less attention. There is a lack of understanding of the functions that security sectors perform in reform contexts. Yet, as the cases outlined in Chapter 2 illustrate, attempts at reform are problematic unless accompanied by a strategy to make them meaningful and worthwhile to the specific context in question. As Lieutenant General Abizaid, Chief of the Joint Staff, Pentagon states: 'We want to go in and move too quickly to build western institutions without taking other softer issues into account.'[1] He points out that while there are academic discussions of these soft issues, careful thinking about them is lacking in policy and implementation. Specific issue areas where further research would be of assistance in planning external SSR operations include the proliferation of shadow networks and the foundations that enable the diversity of security institutions that the cases illustrate to exist.

Maximise Institutional Expertise through Increased Cooperation

The need for increased cooperation is a common recommendation for most types of policy improvement. The holistic character of SSR means that it is both essential and sorely lacking. The breadth of the SSR agenda means that there is room for a diverse array of institutions and donors to participate in external assistance operations, as they have done in cases to date. However, the particular expertise that institutions have is often wasted in reform implementation. There has been no systematic consideration of which institutions are best suited to which parts of security reform, or which donors are best positioned to influence institutional change. There is a need to break down the SSR agenda into its respective parts, consider who is best situated to undertake them and then put the parts back together again. This is a process that may be required for each SSR context. While such an effort may be time consuming and costly initially, as the lack of operational coherence to date demonstrates, the payoffs once implementation is underway could be considerable.

Appreciate Political Constraints Affecting Reform Contexts from the Outset and Sequence Reform Operations Accordingly

Finally, when planning for reform there is a need to be more frank about the political constraints that may characterise reform contexts. The struggles for statehood, as the cases of Palestine and East Timor illustrate, have often jeopardised attempts to implement comprehensive security reforms. In the case of Bosnia, as is quite typical of peace implementation settings, a key constraint upon the development of a comprehensive framework for security reform is the need to establish immediate stability. It remains very difficult to reconcile the demands for stability with the need to develop measures that will assist in long-term security consolidation. More generally, SSR proposals are often characterised by challenges to some aspects of political or state legitimacy that makes leaders extremely reluctant to relinquish or redistribute control of security.

Despite these constraints, external reformers tend to remain attached to the ideal of achieving holistic reforms. As a consequence, there is a reluctance to think about how SSR could be sequenced more effectively: undertaking some parts of the SSR agenda in the early stages of external assistance operations, while delaying others until the political context has changed. Framing reform, establishing where reform is to take place, and what is and what is not included within the policy boundaries will set the parameters, not only of the breadth and depth of involvement, but also for credible change. Reformers are unlikely to be able to do everything at once and an appreciation of the consequences of only addressing some things some of the time may contribute to a more coordinated, thought-through policy. If the political will for particular SSR measures is lacking, then it is unlikely that they will succeed. Whether or not external actors could or should play a role in influencing that political will depends upon the context in question, and the approaches taken during SSR implementation.

Initiating Reform: Establishing Local Ownership

As Forster argues, 'Self-help remains a central aspect determining the embeddedness of reform. It cannot be imposed from the outside.'[2] Alvaro de Soto, Senior Political Advisor to the Secretary-General and principal negotiator during the 1990–1992 negotiations that led to the peace accords between the Salvadoran government and the FMLN, makes a similar point: 'the international community cannot effectively impose national institutions on nations.'[3] This poses a number of challenges when it comes to engaging in reform, challenges which have thus far not been adequately addressed.

Do Not Rely on Conditionality

There have been numerous attempts to bridge the imposition-ownership divide. Most involve the use of conditionality. When conditionality is tied to long-term political objectives – when leverage is at its greatest – such as with the candidate countries for membership of the EU or NATO, the chances of influencing SSR are at their greatest. However, in the majority of reform contexts, incentives do not hold such significant stakes. By making economic assistance conditional on declarations of support for the SSR agenda, donors can get governments to sign on to a process. However, as Chalmers explains, 'it is much more difficult to get a government to genuinely believe in reform in its own right, to participate in its design and to be ready to continue it when external interest is exhausted.'[4] Not least, one always needs to be aware of reform programmes being seen by recipients as simply mechanisms for the extraction of resources from donors.

Moreover a conditionality-based approach is not necessarily consistent with long-term efforts to strengthen governance, i.e. local capacity to formulate and implement policy more effectively. Creating an enabling environment for reform in which security decision-making can occur in a more open and effective manner is crucial if public sector management principles such as accountability are to be put into practice. Yet, as the cases discussed in Chapter 2 illustrate, a redistribution of security will require the development, from virtually bottom up, of an appropriate institutional framework. This will not be achieved without substantive involvement and understanding with both social values and organisational practices, a domain where the rationale of donors may be quite different to that of recipients. The asymmetrical relationship that conditionality implies is therefore not only hard to sustain, it is also problematic in its basic assumptions, and potentially silences a range of local actors, their needs and independent potential to take initiatives. The latter quality of reform contexts in particular is one aspect all too often overlooked by external reformers.

Pay More Attention to the Relationship Between Local Reform Initiatives and External Security Assistance

External assessments of local potential to establish more inclusive security relationships appear to be based on a blinkered view of just what is and is not possible in a given society. A deeper understanding of internally driven security reform has much to offer in terms of reassessing the potential for security change in societies where security is still exclusive or divisive. Writing about Indonesia, and despite the security changes in other South-east Asian states, Huxley comments: 'There is little acknowledgement of the potential for indigenous political development, specifically the growth of civil society, the related impetus for constitutional reform and the establishment of democratic norms and practices to motivate SSR.' Citing the examples of Cambodia, Indonesia and East Timor, he concludes: 'one policy implication is clear from the three examples of external assistance ... more could be done in the vital area of enhancing the oversight capacity of civilian bodies – whether parliaments, the public service, the media or NGOs.'[5] A similar point could be made about the vast majority of cases targeted for reform.

Local reform initiatives are not as scarce as external donors sometimes assume. The problems that external reformers encounter in terms of the competition between alternative security traditions and newly introduced institutions, set out in Chapter 2, can also be seen as a reflection of the ability of reform contexts to foster change. It is therefore surprising that these local mechanisms often remain undiscovered or are ignored in declared SSR policy.

For example, by supervising, advising and when necessary assisting recently deployed forces, UN Observer Mission in El Salvador (ONUSAL) facilitated the creation of El Salvador's post-conflict police force, the National Civilian Police (PNC). ONUSAL police also provided feedback about the PNC's performance to the police training academy. The UN has closely monitored the development of the PNC and used its political leverage when possible. However, by fulfilling this role, ONUSAL created a level of dependency on the UN forestalling the creation of a mechanism for self-evaluation and self-correction by Salvadoran authorities. Meanwhile, the government has been able to subvert the PNC with ex-soldiers largely because of the absence of a robust means for verifying compliance.[6] SSR policy needs to give local initiatives the space to develop their own mechanisms for security change.

That such a local verification mechanism could have been established in the case of El Salvador is given credence by the work of local NGOs. For example, while the immediate effect of ONUSAL's presence was to prevent or dissuade further human rights violations, the human rights component of ONUSAL also effectively displaced – although unintentionally – the human rights work previously carried out by local NGOs and the Catholic Church. ONUSAL has failed to work with these organisations to redefine their roles in the post-war period.[7]

In addition, external assistance in SSR has frequently overridden local processes simply by not taking local conditions into account. When the Office of Transition Initiatives in the USAID decided to help the government of Sierra Leone think through its requirements in the security sector in 1998, it attempted to employ a computer-based methodology more appropriate for making decisions about military hardware acquisition than resolving serious political differences. It also ignored a regional consultant's report outlining in some detail a locally-driven process for decision-making.[8] Consequently, external involvement in the peace process has marginalised civil society groups in Sierra Leone, which formerly were active.

When Possible, Build on What Exists Locally

SSR has been most successful where local initiatives for reform have been supported. South Africa provides the most vivid example of the utilisation of local social security power structures in security reform. The post-apartheid South African security strategy seeks to reproduce a set of structures and processes that accomplish what apartheid accomplished in the past, namely, the mobilisation of a range of government and civilian resources into a functioning security network.[9] The security objective is very different, but the means being utilised are similar.

The White Paper on Safety and Security in South Africa emphasises community crime prevention. This depends upon communities taking responsibility for crime prevention in their own neighbourhoods – a feature that was already common in apartheid times – in parallel with state police forces. Programmes involve the mobilisation of a variety of interest groups to address security on a town or city basis and include a range of concerns in tune with the priorities of a specific area, ranging from improving surveillance through schemes such as car guards or community marshals, to upgrading the role of local communities in preventing domestic violence and child abuse. In addition, civil society groups, such as religious institutions, NGOs, business and community-based organisations and trade unions play a key role in resourcing local social crime prevention programmes.[10] For example, the business community 'buys' police protection in exchange for capital investments in vehicles and buildings. Donations of vehicles and buildings are negotiated with local police in exchange for giving priority to areas of policing that business regards as important.[11]

Don't Fall Back on Imposition

If, having thoroughly explored all of the possibilities described above, imposition is really the only option when implementing reform, then SSR may not be an option at all.

Sustaining Reform: Consolidating Local Ownership
Strengthen Dialogue Between Social Reform and State-led Security Reform Initiatives

Strengthening the interface between social initiatives and government security initiatives has been a key element in the consolidation of security change in South Africa. While civil society had largely been excluded from defence and security debates during the apartheid era, after 1990 locally based research-oriented groups became important players in policy debates, including NGOs such as Ceasefire Campaign, the Institute for Defence Policy (now the Institute for Security Studies which provides consultants to government departments such as the Ministry of Defence and the Ministry of Safety and Security to help develop policies relating to military and police reform), and the Military Research Group, an ANC-aligned think-tank on defence policy.[12]

In certain South-east Asian countries, the increasing and largely internally driven political influence of civil society has also substantially reduced the autonomy of the security establishment, particularly with regards to judicial legislation. During the 1990s in Thailand, pressure from the public, lawyers and the media mounted for an end to extra-judicial killings. Legislation governing inquest procedures, passed in mid-2000, is expected to reduce the frequency of such killings. Another initiative has aimed to reduce the role of police personnel as 'hired guns' for *chao pao*.

Local initiatives are the most important drivers for reform in Nigeria. The National Orientation Agency of Nigeria (NOA) has embarked on creating people's parliaments in some states. In Lagos state, for example, the NOA organised public fora where local government councillors and chairmen gave account of their stewardship. Increasingly, elected members have appeared in public and on private televisions and radios for live discussions. For the first time, the Nigerian public achieved access to contribute to dialogue with public officers about their security concerns without fear while a new role has been established for the press and media.[13]

Enhance Oversight Capacity Through the Development of Dialogue and Knowledge-sharing About SSR

Not all cases are as well poised or proactive in maintaining locally driven reform as those of South Africa and parts of South-east Asia. In El Salvador, as discussed in Chapter 2, support for reform has failed to be matched by the development of specific reform proposals and public discussion remains at a superficial level. Writing about Latin America generally, Mendelson states: 'Civilians ... still remain unschooled on security issues. Creating a role for civilian expertise, developing the mechanisms necessary to train civilians and guaranteeing that those trained will become the planners for the next generation are all necessary steps.'[14] In the meantime, military experts who are part of the armed forces continue to play the dominant role in policy formulation in the ministries.

In Cambodia media coverage of security issues is extremely limited and few non-CPP politicians are sufficiently literate in security matters to challenge the party's line convincingly. Despite the myriad local NGOs in the country there is a distinct shortage of NGO capacity or cooperation in security-related matters. The report on the options for East Timor's post-independence security forces, produced by King's College London's Centre for Defence Studies in August 2000, emphasises the importance of introducing checks and balances to ensure that civil–military relations develop in an appropriate way and argues that 'more work needs to be done by the International Community in East Timor, international and local NGOs and the Transitional Administration – to address the range of issues involved.' The core mechanism suggested by the report is the building of civilian capacity to monitor the security sector, particularly the Defence Force.[15]

In such cases, once reform has been initiated it is important to continue to enhance the oversight capacity of socially based actors. Creating public debate and expertise about security issues, for example through Public Access Networks for Knowledge, is a crucial part of external engagement in security reform, not only in terms of establishing security dialogue and debate, but also in terms of monitoring security change and redefining that change as necessary over time. According to Major General Le Roux, Chief Director of Strategy and Planning in the South African Department of Defence: 'Today the South African defence debate is truly open and enriched by the contributions coming form the Civil Society Organisations.' However, he continues, 'Civil society organisations can only play a role in the defence debate if they are knowledge-able and experts within their own fields. In the South African case this was the reality and it greatly enhanced the debate. Civil society must be involved in the defense debate but must ensure that it has the expertise to do so.'[16]

Huxley puts forward a number of suggestions for improving security expertise and dialogue in societies where debate is lacking. These include providing practical courses in security studies and defence administration through collaboration between foreign and local universities; organising exchange visits by legislators to equivalent parliamentary committees in other countries; and the training of civilian defence experts. Where the first steps towards building up civilian security expertise and dialogue through exter-nal assistance have been taken, the early signs are encouraging. In East Asia, 'second track' institutes and individuals often make an important contribution to developing new ideas for national and regional security policy. Through dialogue mechanisms associated with ASEAN and the ASEAN Regional Forum, they provide a means of testing out new ideas and spreading best practice. Their roles include the provision of advice to governments, parliamentar-ians, and media on security-related issues; regular publications on security issues; and the provision of a forum for national and regional discussions.

Identify Indicators to Assess and Keep Track of Reform

As reform projects are being sustained it is also important to find a means of assessing how successfully SSR is being implemented. The judiciary and its functioning can also act as a key indicator of just what has and has not changed in the security relationships within a society – one way of tracking the success or sustainability of reform. For example, in what was seen locally as an unprecedented test for the traditionally corrupt and inefficient judicial system in Guatemala, the trial took place of three military officers, a priest and a housekeeper for the 1998 killing of Bishop Juan Gerardi. The cleric, who was a veteran human rights activist and long-term critic of the military, was killed in April 1998, two days after releasing a damning report on army abuses against civilians during the 36-year civil war that ended in December 1996. The killing was widely seen as a reprisal from army hardliners. After almost three years of investigations, dogged by constant threats to prosecutors, investigators and witnesses, the case at last reached the courts and the officers were convicted of murder. The three officers convicted include the former head of military intelligence, the highest-ranking officer to be charged in a civilian court in Guatemala's history. According to a lawyer working for a human rights group in Guatemala, 'The Gerardi case has demonstrated that it is possible to do certain things that, in the past, people might have been forgiven for throwing up their hands and saying "these things are not possible here"... The indications are that to some extent the courts are slowly, very, very slowly regaining some form of independence and autonomy.'[17] In early June 2001, the Guatemala City-based Centre for Legal Action on Human Rights (CALDH), representing 12 Mayan communities, went on to file a genocide case against General Efraín Ríos Montt and the military high command for the deaths of 1200 highland villagers during the 'scorched earth' campaign.

Other important indicators are the various media outlets. The discussions in newspapers and on the radio and television can serve as useful indicators of just what the state–society security relationship looks like at a given point in time.

Manage Corruption

The relationship between corruption and security has received the least attention in SSR engagement to date. While it is acknowledged as a challenge to security change, and an impediment to strengthening security institutions and state capacity, it is not something that reformers have purposefully engaged with or used their initiative to tackle. South Africa is perhaps the exception, with the Balkans and certain African states forming perhaps the ultimate, yet most compelling challenge.

As the examples of shadow networking described in Chapter 2 illustrate, corruption can be a key impediment to a process of sustained SSR. All societies practice corruption. However, within some, corruption is endemic: virtually every action and association is dependent upon an unofficial transaction or affiliation. Corruption is a means of getting things done. The important distinction to make is whether corruption is discriminatory or all-encompassing. Do only certain parts of society benefit from corruption at the expense of certain others? Does corruption have an impact upon security relationships and institutions that weakens their ability to provide security for society as a whole? In some cases, the two forms may overlap within a society: in certain circumstances corruption may be all encompassing, in others highly discriminatory. The approach to the two forms of corruption when it comes to engaging with their management is different, but once again involves working from the bottom up.

South African legislation to protect whistle-blowers in the context of anti-corruption initiatives represents an example of how discriminatory corruption is managed. South Africa's transition from apartheid has been characterised by high levels of crime, including widespread corruption. Several initiatives have been undertaken to fight corruption by promoting accountability. These include establishing specialised bodies such as the Special Investigative Unit, hosting anti-corruption conferences since November 1998, as well as passing legislation such as the Promotion of Access to Information Act and the Protected Disclosures Act (no. 26 of 2000) that makes provision for procedures in terms of which employees in both the public and private sector who disclose information of unlawful or corrupt conduct by their employers or fellow employees are protected from losing their jobs, or being demoted. One of the key obstacles in the fight against corruption is the fact that, without such legal protection, individuals are often too intimidated to speak out on corrupt activities that they observe in the workplace. These initiatives depend upon the fact that certain members of society are benefiting at the expense of certain others. Where these boundaries do not exist or are not so clear-cut, this approach is unlikely to work.[18]

If corruption is of the second type – endemic – whereby there is something for everybody to gain or at least opportunity for many parts of a society to benefit, a different approach to the problem may prove more effective. Writing about the shadow networks of Bosnia, Cox argues that: 'In such a case, the priority for an international mission must be to identify and progressively eliminate extra-constitutional sources of power, gradually reducing the war-time regimes down to ordinary political parties.'[19] However, as the tenacity of these networks illustrates, elimination may be impossible.

More importantly, shadow networks perhaps condemned as inherently negative in their effects, need to be rethought and viewed in a more imaginative light. They may in fact be the only structures uniting an otherwise divided society and security system. They are potentially, therefore, a very valuable asset when it comes to assisting security change. For example, the mafiosi of the Balkans provide employment and represent the most multi-ethnic institution in the region. Despite the security divisions manifest at a formal institutional level, when it comes to corruption, society in the Balkans is remarkably cohesive. Switching these interests and energies into another channel, or at least introducing different activities into the same structures through flexible, context-specific incentives could bring previously divided social groups together at the level of security, as well as material gain.

Report and Publish Lessons Learned

Finally, security sector reformers themselves could assist considerably in the quest for engagement by reporting and publishing their own experiences in operations. While there is much material about programme outlines, there is much less useful and frank feedback about operational experiences, and specific problems faced in reform contexts. The systematic consideration of lessons learned by the diverse array of actors involved in SSR operations could enhance the debate considerably.

Conclusion

The most commonly levelled criticism of the SSR agenda – that it is a laudable but fundamentally flawed policy because it is in danger of being based on a partial understanding of the role of the security sector in many parts of the world – remains valid.[1] However, by looking beneath this weakness and understanding its origins, it is also possible to consider how the SSR agenda can be moved beyond the impasse between its laudable objectives and the contextual reality that it faces on the ground, between concept and practice.

Operationally, therefore, SSR cannot only involve a destination. Rather it is the process and route that are all important. This conclusion is supported by the characteristics or circumstances in which reform is attempted. They typically comprise a political context in which strategic priorities are a long way from being focused upon the rights and security of its citizens, where civil society is divided and silenced when it comes to open security debate, and where shadow networks are predators on formal security institutions. Even so, some form of security still exists, albeit in a much more diverse and multi-focal manner than outside analysts sometimes appreciate. For in disputed states there are multiple and often conflicting claims to security that demand numerous orders that are constantly being renegotiated in order to survive. These alternative traditions or cultures as they are commonly viewed, are therefore remarkably tenacious. But they are not immutable and can be of potential value to external assistance in SSR.

As internally driven security reform examples illustrate, local security mechanisms can act to buttress political change and even assist in that change. Most importantly, they have a key role to play in sustaining and maintaining change and even in building institutional capacity. For external reformers, this is the pivotal security interface that provides the mechanisms and ideas for change. It is also the starting point for assessing if it is possible or useful to try to become involved in supporting security change. For SSR is as much about understanding and identifying the limitations of external assistance, as it is the opportunities.

Whatever the intentions of external assistance, experience has shown that security will be determined largely by the society itself. The onus lies on reformers to understand and engage with the society to the extent that is possible. Yet knowing when not to engage is as important as knowing how to engage when the opportunities arise. The entry point for reformers is therefore two-sided: it depends upon their being able to frame reform and look for opportunities, but equally opportunities must be there in the first place, even if the chances of success appear slim or out of reach. This is what the debate about ownership and imposition means, not whether the SSR agenda at its heart is a neo-imperialistic crusade.

Where there is the most potential for ownership, a tangible means and desire for society to support and maintain security change, the prospects for external support are their highest. Where these means or commitment are absent – really absent, as opposed to being overruled or ignored – then externally driven SSR may not be possible until fundamental political change occurs. If there exists ways in which external supporters of reform can support (yet not dominate) locally-led processes of fundamental political change, then this can be a first step towards a process of sustainable SSR. If reformers seek to impose SSR in an inhospitable local environment, however, there are likely to be few, if any, returns.

Notes

Acknowledgement

The author would like to acknowledge the generous help of Dr Yezid Sayigh and Dr Malcolm Chalmers who commented extensively on earlier drafts of this paper.

Introduction

1. Based upon a definition given by Malcolm Chalmers, 'Security Sector Reform in Developing Countries: An EU Perspective', Saferworld and Conflict Prevention Network, January 2000.
2. Malcolm Chalmers, 'Structural Impediments to Security Sector Reform', unpublished paper presented to IISS/GCDCAF conference, Geneva, 23 April 2001.
3. It should be noted that these categories of cases are not mutually exclusive.

Chapter 1

1. WOLA, 'Demilitarising Public Order', November 1995.
2. These provisions were reiterated in the final document, as expressed in Act 108 of 1996.
3. Christopher Smith, 'Mapping the Landscape: The State of Security Sector Reform in the New Millennium', paper presented at the Fourth International Security Forum, workshop on *Civil–Military and Security Sector Reform*, Geneva, 15–17 November 2000.
4. Author's interview with Omar Bakhet, Director, Emergency Response Division, UNDP, New York, November 2000.
5. 'Supplement to An Agenda for Peace', A/50/60–5/1995/1, 3 January 1995, para 47.
6. Report of the Secretary-General on 'The Causes of Conflict and the Promotion of Durable Peace and Sustainable Development in Africa', 1998, para 2.
7. SEECAP, 30 May 2001, Hungary, NATO update, meeting on security issues in southeastern Europe, June 2001.
8. Declaration on the SEECAP on Regional Security Challenges and Opportunities, Budapest, Hungary, 30 May 2001.
9. NATO Parliamentary Assembly, 30 May, 2001.
10. Ian A. Johnson, Vice-President of the World Bank, in the foreword to *World Bank Annual Report 1999*.
11. The World Bank's Experience in Post-Conflict Reconstruction (5 volumes), Washington DC, Operations Evaluations

Department, 4 May 1998, vol. 1, p. 9; Policy Framework on Post-Conflict Reconstruction, Washington DC, The World Bank, 1998.

[12] 'Initiatives in Legal and Judicial Reform', World Bank, 2001.

[13] USAID, Involvement in Post-conflict Reconstruction, April 1997.

[14] Johanna Mendelson Forman and Claude Welch, 'Civil–Military Relations: USAID's Role', July 1998.

[15] Nicole Ball, 'Spreading Good Practices in Security Sector Reform: Policy Options for the British Government', Overseas Development Council, November 1998.

[16] DFID, policy statement, 1997.

[17] Nicole Ball and Tammy Halevy, 'Making Peace Work: The Role of the International Development Community', policy essay no. 18, (Washington DC: Overseas Development Council, 1996).

[18] Damian Lilly, 'The Privatisation of Security and Peacebuilding: a Framework for Action', International Alert, September 2000, p. 23.

[19] Deutsche Gesellschaft fur Technische Zusammenarbeit, Division 43, 'Security-Sector Reform in Developing Countries', Eschborn 2000, p. 21.

[20] Nicole Ball, 'Spreading Good Practices in Security Sector Reform: Policy Options for the British Government', Saferworld, December 1998.

[21] Malcolm Chalmers, 'Security Sector Reform in Developing Countries: an EU Perspective', London: Saferworld and Brussels: Conflict Prevention Network, January 2000.

[22] 'Prevention of Violent Conflict and the Coherence of EU Policies Towards the Horn of Africa', a joint report by InterAfrica Groups and Saferworld, October 2000.

[23] Secretary of State for International Development, Clare Short, speech at the Centre for Defence Studies, King's College London: 'Security Sector Reform and the Elimination of Poverty', 9 March 1999.

[24] Deutsche Gesellschaft fur Technische Zusammenarbeit, Division 43, 'Security-Sector Reform in Developing Countries', Eschborn 2000, p. 15. My italics.

[25] Dylan Hendrickson, Report of 4 April 2000 to the Development Assistance Committee of the OECD.

[26] Malcolm Chalmers, 'Structural impediments to Security Sector Reform', unpublished paper presented to IISS/Centre for the Democratic Control of Armed Forces conference, Geneva, 23 April 2001.

Chapter 2

[1] Fred Tanner, 'Security Sector Reform: Lessons from Bosnia and Herzegovina', unpublished paper presented to IISS/GCDCAF Conference, Geneva, 23 April 2001.

[2] Marcus Cox, 'State Building and Post-conflict Rehabilitation: The Lessons of Bosnia', 4th ISF, Geneva, 15–17 November 2000.

[3] Tanner, 'Security Sector Reform: Lessons from Bosnia and Herzegovina', Geneva, 23 April 2001.

[4] Bertil Linter, 'East Timor: Can It Stand Alone?' *Jane's Intelligence Review*, November 2000, pp. 41–43.

[5] Neil MacFarlane, 'Security Sector Reform in Georgia', unpublished paper presented to IISS/GCDCAF Conference, Geneva, 23 April 2001.

[6] Zoran Kusovac, 'Serbian Security forces in disarray', *Jane's Intelligence Review*, vol. 12, no. 12, December 2000, p. 2.

7 John Schindler, 'Yugoslav Revolution Under Threat', *Jane's Intelligence Review*, January 2001, pp. 18–20.

8 Terence Lee, 'The Nature and Future of Civil–Military Relations in Indonesia', *Asian Survey*, vol. 40, no. 4, 2000, pp. 692–706.

9 John Haseman and Robert Karniol, 'Country Briefing: Indonesia', *Jane's Defence Weekly*, 29 August 2001, pp. 20–26.

10 Alice Hills, 'Defence Diplomacy and Security Sector Reform', *Contemporary Security Policy*, vol. 21, no. 1, April 2000, pp. 46–67, p. 53.

11 A. De Waal, 'Contemporary Warfare in Africa: Changing Context, Changing Strategies', *Institute for Development Studies Bulletin*, vol. 27, no. 3 (Brighton: University of Sussex, Institute for Development Studies, 1996).

12 WOLA, 'Demilitarising Public Order', The International Community, Police Reform and Human Rights in Central America and Haiti', Panel I: The International Community and Police Reform, the United States, November 1995.

13 Kees Koonings, 'Political Armies, Security Forces, and Democratic Consolidation: Comparative Observations with Particular Reference to the Latin American Experience', Utrecht University, Notes for the Workshop, Security Structures and Democratic Governance, University of Witwatersrand, 17–20 September 2000.

14 Mark Shaw and Clifford Shearing, 'Reshaping Security: An Examination of the Governance of Security in South Africa', *African Security Review*, vol. 7, no. 3, 1998.

15 ibid.

16 Said Adejumobi, 'Demilitarisation and Democratic Re-orientation in Nigeria: Issues, Problems and Prospects', *Verfassung und Recht in Ubersee* (VRU), no. 33, 2000.

17 ibid.

18 Christopher Clapham, 'African Security Systems: Privatisation and the Scope for Mercenary Activity', in Greg Mills and John Stremlau (eds.), *The Privatisation of Security in Africa* (Johannesburg: The South African Institute of International Affairs in association with the US Institute of Peace, March, 1999), p. 24.

19 Eboe Hutchful, 'Understanding the Africa Security Crisis', in Abdel Fatau Musah and J. Kayode Fayemi (eds.), *Mercenaries: An African Security Dilemma* (London: Pluto Press, 1999), p. 213.

20 Emmanuel Kwesi Aning, 'Ghana Election 2000: Implications and Significance for the Future', *Africa Security Review*, vol. 10, no. 2, 2001, pp. 37–48, pp. 44–45.

21 Somalia, IRIN Special – Establishing the interim government, UN OCHA, 16 October 2000.

22 Ameen Jan, 'Peacebuilding in Somalia', International Peace Academy Policy Briefing Series, New York, IPA, 1996.

23 Shaw and Shearing, 'Reshaping Security', vol. 7, no. 3, 1998.

24 See Damian Lilly, 'The Privatisation of Security and Peacebuilding: a Framework for Action', International Alert, Septermber 2000.

25 Marc-Antoine Perouse de Montclos, 'Does Africa Need the Police?', *Le Monde Diplomatique*, September 1997.

26 MacFarlane, 'Security Sector Reform in Georgia', Geneva, 23 April 2001.

27 WOLA, 'Demilitarising Public Order II: Peace Processes and Reform: El Salvador and Nicaragua, Nicaragua, November 1995.

28 Office of the High Representative

speech to the UNSC, New York, 8 November 1999.

[29] *ibid.*

[30] See OHR: Property Legislation; OHR: Decisions by the High Representative, OHR: Media Restructuring in Bosnia Herzegovina.

[31] OHR speech to the UNSC, New York, 8 November 1999.

[32] MacFarlane, 'Security Sector Reform in Georgia', Geneva, 23 April 2001; James Sherr, 'Security Sector Reform in the Ukraine: A Comparative Perspective', unpublished paper presented to IISS/GCDCAF Conference, Geneva, 23 April 2001.

[33] Adejumobi, 'Demilitarisation and Democratic Re-orientation in Nigeria', VRU, no. 33 (2000).

[34] Emmanuel Kwesi Aning, 'Ghana Election 2000: Implications and Significance for the Future', *Africa Security Review*, vol. 10, no. 2, 2001. 'The Ghana Governance and Corruption Survey: Evidence from Households, Enterprises and Public Officials', World Bank and Ghana Centre for Democratic Governance, CDD, Accra, August 2000.

[35] John Schindler, 'Bosnia Prepares for Life after Izetbegovic', *Jane's Intelligence Review*, February 2001, pp. 25–27.

[36] Zoran Kusovac, 'New Rivals Protect Old Guard,' *Jane's Intelligence Review*, March 2001, pp. 17–19.

[37] Testimony before the Committee on International Relations, House of Representatives, United States General Accounting Office, Bosnia: Crime and Corruption Threaten Successful Implementation of the DPA, Statement of Harold J. Johnson.

[38] John Schindler, 'Yugoslav Revolution Under Threat', *Jane's Intelligence Review*, January 2001, pp. 18–20.

[39] Patrick Chabal, 'Africa in the Age of Globalisation', *African Security Review*, vol. 10, no. 2, 2001, p. 112.

[40] CPN Western Balkans Final Security Report, March 2000, Stiftung Wissenschaft und Politik, pp. 19–21.

[41] GTZ, 'Security Sector Reform in Developing Countries', October 2000, p. 34.

[42] Sherr, 'Security Sector Reform in the Ukraine', Geneva, 23 April 2001.

[43] Tim Huxley, 'Security Sector Reform in Southeast Asia', unpublished paper presented to IISS/GCDCAF Conference, Geneva, 24 April 2001.

[44] Gavin Cawthra, 'Civil Society and the State in South Africa: Past Legacies, Present Realities, and Future Prospects', p. 12. 'Security Transformation in Post-apartheid South Africa', discussion at workshop on Security Structures and Good Governance, University of Witwatersrand, Johannesburg, 18–20 September 2000.

[45] Fred Tanner, 'Security Sector Reform: Lessons from Bosnia and Herzegovina', IISS/GCDCAF Conference, Geneva, 23 April 2001.

[46] Adejumobi, 'Demilitarisation and Democratic Re-orientation in Nigeria', VRU, no. 33 (2000).

[47] WOLA, 'Demilitarising Public Order', Panels I and II, November, 1995.

[48] *ibid.*

[49] Dylan Hendrickson, 'A Review of Security-Sector Reform', *The Conflict, Security and Development Group*, working paper no. 1, September 1999.

[50] *ibid.*

[51] Alice Hills, 'Defence Diplomacy and Security Sector Reform', *Contemporary Security Policy*, vol. 21, no. 1, April 2000, pp. 46–67, p. 52.

[52] Mary Kaldor, *New and Old Wars:*

Organized Violence in a Global Era, (Stanford, CA: Stanford University Press, 1999), p. 131.

53 Susan L. Woodward, 'Security and the Stability Pact', presentation at first annual meeting of SEEPIN, Ohrid, Macedonia, 23–25 June 2000.

54 Juan Pekmez, 'The Intervention by the International Community and the Rehabilitation of Kosovo', 4th International Security Forum, Geneva, 15–17 November 2000.

Chapter 3

1 Interview with Lieutenant General Abizaid, Chief of the Joint Staff, Pentagon, Washington DC, 1 December 2000.

2 Anthony Forster, 'Civil–Military and Security Sector Reform: West Looking East', paper prepared for the Workshop on 'Civil–Military Relations and Security Sector Reform' at the 4th International Security forum, 14–17 November 2000.

3 WOLA, Demilitarising Public Order, Panel I, November 1995.

4 Malcolm Chalmers, 'Structural Impediments to Security Sector Reform', unpublished paper presented to IISS/GCDCAF Conference, Geneva, 23 April 2001.

5 Tim Huxley, 'Security Sector Reform in Southeast Asia', IISS/GCDCAF Conference, Geneva, 24 April 2001.

6 David H. McCormick, 'From Peacekeeping to Peacebuilding: Restructuring Military and Police Institutions in El Salvador', in Michael W. Doyle, Ian Johnstone, Robert C. Orr (eds), *Keeping the Peace* (UK: Cambridge University Press, 1997), pp. 282–311, p. 305.

7 David Holiday and William Stanley, 'Building the Peace: Preliminary lessons from El Salvador', *Journal of International Affairs*, vol. 46, no. 2, Winter 1993, pp. 415–438.

8 Nicole Ball, ODC, 'The Role and Problems of International Assistance in Support of Democratic Control of the Military and Security Establishments', prepared for roundtable on 'Democratic Control of Military and Security Establishments in Nigeria and South Africa', 20–23 September 2000, Centre for Security and Defence Management, University of Witwatersrand, Johannesburg.

9 Etienne Marias and Janine Rauch, 'Policing South Africa: Reform and Prospects', paper presented at IDASA Conference: Policing in South Africa in the 1990s, Van der Bijl Park, October 1992.

10 Janine Rauch, 'The Limits of Police Reform', CSVR, Indicator SA, vol. 8, no. 4, Spring 1991, pp. 17–20.

11 Shaw and Shearing, 'Reshaping Security', vol. 7, no. 3, 1998.

12 Cawthra, 'Security Transformation in Post-Apartheid South Africa', University of Witwatersrand, Johannesburg, 18–20 September 2000.

13 Gani Joses Yoroms, 'Strengthening Mechanisms for Democratic Accountability and Control in Nigeria', presented at the 2nd roundtable on 'Democratic Control of the Military and Security Establishments in Nigeria and South Africa', Centre for Security and Defence Management, University of Witwatersrand, Johannesburg, 20–22 September 2000.

14 Mendelson Forman and Welch, 'Civil–Military Relations: USAID's Role', July 1998.

15 Independent study on 'Security Force Options and Security Sector Reform for East Timor', London, Centre for Defence Studies, King's College London, August 2000, paras 104–107.

[16] Major-General Len Le Roux, 'Defence Restructuring in the Context of Democratisation: Actors and Issues, paper delivered to the 2nd roundtable on 'Democratic Control of Military and Security Establishments in Nigeria and South Africa, Centre for Defence and Security Management, University of Witwatersrand, Johannesburg, 21 September 2000.

[17] Latin America Monitor: Central America, May 2001.

[18] Lala Camerer, 'Protecting Whistle Blowers in South Africa: The Protected Disclosures Act, no. 26 of 2000', ISS paper 47, January 2001.

[19] Marcus Cox, 'State Building and Post-conflict Rehabilitation: The Lessons of Bosnia', 4th ISF, Geneva, 15–17 November 2000.

Conclusion

[1] Alice Hills, 'Defence Diplomacy and Security Sector Reform', *Contemporary Security Policy*, vol. 21, no. 1, April 2000, pp. 46–67, p. 48.